TERRY SCHMIDA'S
TRUE CRIME
VOL. 3

STORIES OF
KEY WEST
AND THE
FLORIDA KEYS

Cover design and layout:
Danette Baso Silvers of Invites by Danette

Rare first edition. Buy as many copies as you can carry!

ISBN-13: 978-1494381066
ISBN-10: 1494381060

Bigfoot the cat

TABLE OF CONTENTS

For Al, Shane, Andrea, Adri, Freddy,
and all the rest who had to leave the film early . . .

INTRODUCTION

Those closest to me know that at heart I'm suspicious of fiction. I appreciate it as pleasurable reading, but I'm often left wondering which parts were invented purely in the writers' imagination, and which were inspired by true events, people or places that exist but may have been changed, and how and why were they changed, etc. I've just always been drawn to unraveling and peeling back the layers of a story to get to the heart of the truth. It's stranger and more entertaining than fiction. Why dress up reality if you don't need to?

My great-great uncle Myles "The Slasher" Finnan didn't have the luxury of speaking the truth freely. He was an Irish Republican patriotic poet who published his subversive reportage under the guise of such harmless yarns as "An Ode to a Potato" in Dublin, in the watershed year of 1916. He was forced to flee to America where the First Amendment says we can write what we wish.

In 1997 I wished to write about crime. True crime, mind you. No fiction here. The uncut funk. I was inspired by Canadian true crime writer Max Haines of the *Toronto Sun*, to take a job as crime reporter at the *Key West Citizen* that year, and it introduced me to a side of Key West history that was fascinating to me. Memorable murders had been touched on here and there in old-timers' self-published bios, and immortalized in song and on the stage, but nobody had undertaken before to present the most interesting and notorious stories in one place. You're now reading my third such volume of Keys true crime stories since 2006.

Return readers will note that, as in the first two books, the tales I've selected jump back and forth in time, from the racially charged trial and execution for rape of Sylvanus Johnson in 1897, to the senseless killing of gentle Key West horticulturalist Rodger Keller in 2006. These stories are generally of more recent vintage than the ones in *Vol. 2*, just as that book is itself a stepping stone in time from *Vol. 1*. Neophytes to the series can work their way back in time with the other books without becoming confused.

In the course of my research I've been struck by the harshness of some of the newer cases. In particular I don't recommend reading

"Monster," "A Dark and Stormy Night," or "Streets of Key West" to small children before bedtime, if ever. The closer this history creeps to our own time, the easier it is to imagine it happening, and to feel revulsion towards the criminals, and empathy for the victims. For this reason, and not in spite of it, I've elected in each book to add a little frivolity to the mix, in the spirit of "The Producers." This is done not to demean the suffering of the victims at the hands of their despicable tormentors, but to help keep perspective of how rare violent crimes are in the Keys, and how we're lucky to sometimes even enjoy a guilty chuckle or two over a non-violent offender with a sense of humor.

This book is not a glorification of violence; the reading of "Streets" in fact, might help prevent it. It is, however, a glorification of Keys' humor.

On March 5, 2010, those of us who toil in the *Citizen* newsroom had a collective belly laugh, when Upper Keys resident Megan Mariah Barnes caused a two-car collision at Mile Marker 21 on Cudjoe Key. (No one was injured.) It turned out that Barnes was on her way to meet her new boyfriend and was trying to drive while, er . . . shaving. Her ex-husband was holding the steering wheel. The day before she had been convicted of DUI and driving with her license suspended. At the time of the accident, she was on probation and had been ordered not to drive for five years.

"I'm really starting to believe this stuff only happens in the Keys," one of the arresting cops had remarked.

The story made the national news, including such TV programs as Letterman and the Daily Show. And it reminded me that it was time to get to work on more top-shelf material for another installment in the series. In the years since the publication of *Vol. 1,* I've done TV, radio, and print interviews with media outlets from all over the world who wanted to hear more about the life and crimes of those of us who live in the Florida Keys. I've also heard from many readers who expressed hopes that I'd be writing another one at some point.

That point has now arrived.

Once more, I give you what you want.

Terry Schmida
December, 2013

THE FLORIDA KEYS

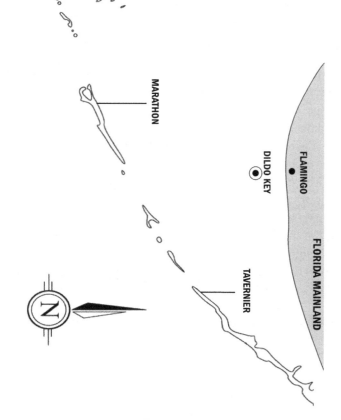

KEY WEST

STOCK ISLAND

BOCA CHICA NAS

BIG COPPITT KEY

BIG PINE KEY

MARATHON

FLAMINGO

DILDO KEY

TAVERNIER

FLORIDA MAINLAND

N

A FOREWARD BY
TOM CORCORAN

You don't have to show a government-issued photo ID to enter paradise, but you might leave with one. Yes, that's another version of the "arrive-on-vacation, depart-on-probation" saying, but aren't clichés born of truth? The facts are clear. Plenty of people screw up in the Florida Keys. They make "bad choices" elsewhere too, but there's a difference. Something about our geography, weather and natural beauty inspires creativity. We get to witness an unending fandango of blissed-out criminal concepts, bizarre deeds, and incredibly stupid escape attempts. This string of islands is where imaginations - both wholesome and damaged - run free.

Why us and why here? Okay, we're in crazy-ass Florida. But way the hell down between Miami and Havana we still stand out. How do we manage to draw so many rookies, fumblers, clumsy thugs, and bad planners? Do mainland judges and parole officers hand out road maps showing the end of the road? Are criminals, like artists, drawn to the ends of peninsulas? Has the heat fried their brains? Is our small corner of paradise a crime magnet? Are we the southernmost downspout for the "funnel of trouble," doomed to welcome every road dog traipsing down U.S. 1?

We definitely attract wanderers and the mentally ill. We draw young runaways and older people who wish to reinvent their lives - men and women dodging lovers, unpaid bills, the law, the general rat race, back taxes, alimony, lost jobs and abuse. If you can't afford the heating bill in Iowa, the better place to be broke is Florida. If life's burdens have chipped away at your sanity, there is nothing as therapeutic as a fair-weather ocean view to provide calm, to peel away dread.

Plus there's the tourism factor. Is there any other town in Florida that's busier at 1 a.m. than it is at 3 p.m.? Key West, for several decades, has provided the party-minded with an open-air bullring, a bar-hop venue where bathing suits after midnight are no big deal, scraped knees are a merit badge, and partial nudity no more out of place than a neon beer sign.

I recall being in New York City on a cold evening, years ago wondering why the people sleeping on steam grates or on benches under folded-out newspapers hadn't found their way to Florida. Why couldn't they find the toasty island where I had lived cheaply through the 1970s - with a roof over my head but not always sure how I would pay for my next month's groceries?

Well, they eventually discovered the warmest place to be homeless. I expect it was word-of-mouth, but the secret didn't come from mine.

They carried in meager possessions and their addictions and psychological wounds and, perhaps, their disaffection with society in general. Not all of them turn to crime, but sometimes rules and statutes take second seat to life's other considerations. Sometimes giving a damn is the last thing people care about.

Some budding criminals reach the Florida Keys with fat wallets. Many are familiar with Greek yogurt and cruise control, rate-of-return and smoked salmon. Why do the financially privileged suddenly flip out or cash it all in? Do they come here so they don't screw up in their home towns? Do they throw it all away because they feel unworthy of their wealth? Do they think they are too big to go down, and their money can buy them out of any trouble? Only philosophers and prison guards know the answers.

Finally, we know that our homegrown long-term residents and true Conchs make plenty of social errors. People who should know the terrible odds, the usual bad endings to shady misadventures. Perhaps this issue is easier to understand by studying the distant past.

A hundred and twenty years ago Florida was a refuge for scoundrels ducking the law, hiding from society. The Keys were part of that but different. Key West was a maritime crossroads with a rough-and-tumble atmosphere. The old days fostered a spirit of coexistence. As in any remote region, there was a tradition of looking the other way. No one had an easy life, and transportation was a challenge, so the townsfolk and the law often ignored victimless crime. Even crimes with genuine victims slipped through the system. If you killed your neighbor on Ramrod Key 60 years ago, you could be vacationing in South America before your victim's body washed up in West Palm Beach. You could return home in a few months and be just as bewildered as everyone else by that neighbor's disappearance. It was a paradise for bad guys too.

As I write this, an unsuccessful bank robber committed his crime and was caught in a matter of several hours. He was known on the island, disguised himself only with sunglasses and failed to account for high-resolution security photos and the power of the Internet. Not all of the stolen money was recovered, so we might assume that he paid back people to whom he owed money then guaranteed himself three meals and a bunk for a few years - which beats weed-sleeping with the skeeters. We'll have to wait for another volume of these heinous tales to get all the facts.

Finally, Key West provides the classic crime novel conflict of wealth and poverty. The island attracts dreamers, and we are left to consider what comes next, what challenges might await the postmodern felon. Now that the Monroe County Sheriff's Office has created "cold case" pages on social media, are there new incentives for criminal activity, for Bonnie-and-Clyde-level fame? The sheriff's mug shot page gets so many hits per week, they've begun to sell advertising. Do current-day perpetrators strive for their place in history, their bad acts going viral? Going one step further, could this book in your hands be reason enough for someone to break the law?

"Honey, I've dreamed up the perfect crime."

"Will it get us into Terry Schmida's *Vol. IV*?"

"Probably, but we might have to buy him a beer or two."

"With our hard-earned ill-gotten gains? To hell with that."

"Maybe it's not so perfect after all."

Tom Corcoran is the author of the Alex Rutledge Series of mystery novels set in the Keys. He also created Key West in Black and White, *a book of 160 photographs taken from 1974 to the late 1990s.*

Photo by roboneal.com

Two shots of Rumrunners bar in happier times.

TWILIGHT

Laid-off nightclub bouncer Jeffrey Wade Wallace claimed he was tormented and bitten by a vampire in a den of evil. His dark retribution reverberates still . . .

Despite its laid-back, blissed-out atmosphere, sunny Key West can be a tough place to live. High rents, low pay and a sense of rootlessness make the situation particularly hard for the stressed-out service industry employees who keep the non-stop cocktail party rolling. Many folks need to work several jobs to make ends meet. Some get chewed up and spat out by the system's unforgiving mandibles, or derailed by drugs and alcohol. Put simply it's not much fun working all the time when everyone around you is on vacation. The idealized 1970s lifestyle depicted in "The Key West Picture Show" has become an out-of-reach mirage for most.

Not surprisingly, all this workplace pressure has manifested itself in some very nasty, and sometimes deadly, confrontations – especially amongst people who may have had mental problems to begin with. Troubled Jeffrey Wade Wallace was one such individual.

● ● ●

As twilight descended on the evening of April 7, 1997, the employees of the Hideaway bar, at the rear of the Duval Street Rumrunners entertainment complex, were getting ready to do it up all over again. The tiny but popular late-night spot with its iconic batwing logo was the only punk rock/grunge club in Key West. It kept hours that might well be described as "vampiric." Which is just the way its mostly local, dusk-to-dawn, clientele liked it. Many overworked bartenders, club musicians, and strippers of a certain age fondly recall the obscure, black-lit dive for its beer-soaked floorboards, cheap drinks, and raging house band N.F.I. A gnarly old tree grew up through the low wooden ceiling.

Keith Richards would have felt right at home there.

Paranoid preacher's son Jeffrey Wade Wallace, who often talked of "evil forces" and sometimes slept with a knife next to his bed, felt differently. In fact the four-year Key West resident would later describe the Hideaway, and the entire Rumrunners complex, as a shadowy netherworld of drugs, prostitution – and Satan-loving vampires – where he feared for his life on a daily basis.

Wallace had recently been let go from his job as a Spring Break bouncer at the bar, but on this particular April night he was back as a customer. He ordered a shot of Jägermeister and downed it. Suspecting that the drink had been watered down Wallace complained about it to the bartender. Then he left.

Shortly after midnight, however, Wallace returned, this time dressed all in black, and armed with a 9 mm semi-automatic Glock pistol. His pockets were stuffed with extra ammunition magazines and dozens of loose rounds.

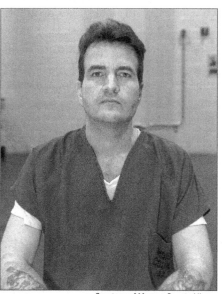
Courtesy of Monroe County Library
Jeffrey Wade Wallace

As patrons drank, laughed and danced to the Devil's own music, the madness began. Wallace stepped up to the bar, drew his gun and "fired in a row at human targets frozen where they stood," the *Key West Citizen* reported on April 9.

Wallace's first shot grazed the head of barkeep Brian Sawyer. The loud crack of gunfire sent patrons ducking to the floor, or dashing toward the exits. Wallace again took aim. His second bullet struck and mortally wounded his former boss, Hideaway General Manager Michael Sumner. Next to be hit was bartender Frank Lapriola, then another Hideaway employee, Michael Francis. Wallace also managed to target a sole customer, Kristin Hutchins of Raleigh, N.C., before several bouncers leaped upon him and wrested the Glock from his hand. Police soon arrived to take the killer into custody.

The attack was over but the heartbreak had just begun.

While Wallace's victims were being rushed to hospital, the shackled shooter sat in a paddy wagon outside the bar giving a statement to Key West Police Officer Robert Winterbottom.

"I would have done more if not stopped," Wallace told Winterbottom. "Young people come down here and get tormented.

They are evil and somebody had to do something. They said they were vampires and I was prepared. I have a tattoo on my left arm of St. Michael the Angel. He rids the world of evil." It sounded straight from a pulp vampire novel. Was Wallace actually nuts or merely laying the groundwork for an insanity plea?

The next day as mourners laid flowers and candles against the now-closed bar's front door, the authorities set about trying to find out.

● ● ●

By early June Assistant State Attorney Manny Madruga, who was to try the case, felt he had his answer. Two out of three psychiatrists who examined the 37-year-old Wallace agreed to varying degrees that he was not insane, per se. After Wallace refused a plea-bargain for a life sentence without parole, Madruga announced that the state would seek the death penalty in the case.

"But for the actions of a few brave individuals, this would have been the worst mass murder in the state of Florida," Madruga told the *Citizen*. "(Wallace's) actions created great risk to many people," given "the premeditated, cold and calculated way the shooting was done."

By now, with Wallace's other victims out of immediate danger, Sumner's former colleagues took time to grieve the loss of the popular manager, whom Rumrunners' co-owner Michael "Mickey" Marone had called "a great kid."

"Mike was a great guy," concurred his former employer, Mike Bloom. "A friendly, all around good guy. He was honest. Had integrity. Everyone liked him."

Just so, the news of the state's decision to seek the ultimate punishment for Wallace came as a relief to Rumrunners' other boss Virginia Paugh, who would have become the slain Michael Sumner's mother-in-law, but for the murderous rampage.

"That's great," she said. "I'm relieved. I was so afraid his charade of insanity would be believed and [the death penalty] wouldn't be happening."

● ● ●

15

Now that Wallace was formerly charged with one count of first-degree murder and four counts of attempted first-degree murder with a firearm, proceedings got underway in the third week of September 1998, in the Key West courtroom of County Judge Mark Jones. A 12-person jury had already been selected, but with Court TV broadcasting the proceedings, the court of public opinion now numbered in the hundreds of millions.

Likewise, with so many witnesses to the events of April 8, 1997, all Wallace's lawyers, Jim Nolan and Patricia Docherty really had to work with was an insanity defense.

"Much of the case will turn on the testimony of laypersons, the non-experts," the *Citizen* reported on Sept. 16.

"The feeling is that since both sides will be providing expert testimony, the experts will cancel each other out," Jim Nolan told the paper.

at tHe tI Me OF tHe cRI Me...

Behind the green door of the Alligator Adult Bookstore on Duval Street a foul deed was committed on the night of July 30, 1996. Intoxicated Key Wester Ed O'Connor wandered into the store and began playing video games in the back room. That's when store employee Kenya Ramsey sneaked up behind him, bashed him in the head twice with a baseball bat, and then stuffed the body into one of the store's porno viewing booths. O'Connor died later in the hospital. The motive for the murder was robbery, which netted Ramsey and his accomplice David Kerlin a grand total of $2. Both men were sentenced to life without the possibility of parole, for committing the senseless crime.

On the first day of the trial, the prosecution opened with a statement describing Wallace as "calm" and "cool" that fateful April night. Even as he was disarmed and detained by Hideaway bouncers, he "continued issuing dire threats to get out of jail, come back and finish what he started," according to the *Citizen*.

Wallace's crime, Manny Madruga said, "was an act of revenge, a crime not of fear but of anger."

The defense countered with an explanation of Wallace's "delusional disorder," which they said had begun following the early death of his sermonizing father. It had become worse, in his late 20s, "spreading like a cancer" and turning the future gunman increasingly paranoid. He had come to Key West to try to get away from this darkness, but it had followed him there, just as it had followed him to California, Memphis, and West Palm Beach before his arrival here.

Nolan disputed the charge that the shooting had been premeditated. "There was no circling on the calendar," he said. The mental problems had, by that point, "totally consumed Jeff's life." The prosecution's own shrink had concluded Wallace suffered from a delusional disorder, he pointed out.

Lastly, Nolan did his best to puncture claims by Wallace's former cellmate that the accused had bragged of his "psychological prowess" and ability to game the system, by pointing out that he had spent less than a week with him, and had mailed some of Wallace's belongings to media outlets.

For their part, Wallace's surviving victims described their brutal ordeal and excruciating injuries sustained that night, as the "smiling gunman" stepped from the darkness to fire a hail of hollow-point bullets at their bodies.

● ● ●

The next day, prosecutors played a tape of the "rambling" 15 minute confession Wallace gave police shortly after his arrest.

"I'm glad I did it," he kept repeating. "I wish I'd killed them all. I'm proud of what I did. They kept [messing] with me. They're [expletive] evil, dude."

Wallace also referred to a girl who bit him at the Hideaway, claiming to be a vampire, and he asserted that Rumrunners' owners had used the Internet to track his movements across the country. A Boston-based Mafia was running drug and prostitution rings out of the bar, Wallace insisted.

Defense attorney Nolan was left asking police witnesses if they were aware of any such illegal activities at the bar, and didn't they think some of the accusations in Wallace's confession should have been looked into?

"I'm sure there are drugs in that area," replied Lt. Al Flowers, "but I'm not aware of any in particular."

By now a year-and-a-half had passed since the shooting and Wallace's time in jail was beginning to show in his waistline. The accused had lost 40 pounds already, by eating less. This was, he stated, out of fear that he was being poisoned by the authorities.

● ● ●

On Sept. 21 an outwardly emotional Wallace took the stand to tell his side of the story.

Working at the Hideaway had been a humiliating, life-threatening experience. Co-workers joked that he was dangerous, calling out "here comes the shooter," as he walked by. "He's going to kill all of us," they would say.

He recalled the "vampire bite" he received from the demon girl at the bar, and of awaking feeling that he had been drugged and beaten. Even house band N.F.I. were intimates in this supposed Satanic circle, according to Wallace, performing a song titled "Bullet in the Head," when he was around. (That the song was actually written by California band Rage Against the Machine, seemed to be beside the point to the shooter.)

"I was no threat to them," Wallace told the court.

Yet he felt threatened in return. The night before the shooting, he said, he smoked a cigarette thinking he might soon be killed.

"It was like smoking my last cigarette before going to the firing squad."

Instead he decided to force the issue.

"Why prolong the agony?" he decided. "Let's get this over with. I would put a stop to all of this. I didn't have a choice."

So Wallace showed up at the bar the next evening to confront his enemies, and the "evil forces" which controlled them, in hopes of getting them to back down.

His "black suit of death" and tattoo of the avenging angel were supposed to "intimidate them [so] they would leave [him] alone." In his head he heard his late father's voice telling him "evil prevails when good men do nothing."

That's when Wallace, "defending himself," began shooting.

Asked by his lawyer what happened next, Wallace replied "Nightmare . . . chaos, some people grabbed me, hit me with a bottle, choking, holding me."

Again prosecutor Madruga inquired what exactly Wallace thought he was defending himself from.

Wallace answered: "The satanic cult and the Boston Mafia."

On Oct. 8, the jury came back after three hours with their verdict: Guilty on all counts.

In the rear of the courtroom, friends and family members of Wallace's victims wept and embraced. Some were less pleased the next day when the same jury surprised them by recommending Wallace be jailed for life without parole, rather than pay for his acts with his life, but the sentence did offer some degree of permanency. Never again would Wallace be in a position to inflict harm on others. He is currently incarcerated at the Cross City Correctional Institution in northern Florida, where he maintains that what he did made perfect sense.

"The best example I can give," Wallace told the *New York Times* in a 2000 interview, "is you're in your house and somebody breaks in and you have to defend yourself and you end up killing somebody. It's terrible but what can you do?"

● ● ●

The final victim of Jeffrey Wade Wallace turned out to be the Hideaway itself. Not long after the trial, the bar was razed and is now a parking lot and occasional venue for special events such as Spring Break wet T-shirt contests.

As with many such former crime scenes around the globe, it's possible to walk past it without gleaning the slightest inkling of the life-altering carnage that time and a bulldozer have helped to obscure. At first it seemed a shame for many regular patrons, including the author, that the bar be lost forever, but on reflection it's probably better this way. It simply would have been impossible to sit in the place without imagining that terrifying night in April of 1997 when evil itself visited the Hideaway . . .

BATTY IN THE KEYS

In February of 2011 a 15-year-old girl told police she had been attacked and bitten all over her body in a vampirish fashion. It turned out the Marathon High Schooler was a fan of the "Twilight" book and film series who had been engaging in "fantasy biting" sessions with two older friends. She was arrested for filing a false police report.

Meanwhile bat lovers in the Keys can visit the Sugarloaf Key Bat Tower near Mile Marker 17. They won't see any vampires, though. The tower was built in 1929 to help control mosquitoes in the Lower Keys but there wasn't enough fresh water in the area to sustain a bat population. Immediately after being placed in the tower the bats bolted, never to be seen again. Florida Keys historian Tom Hambright jokingly suggests that the mosquitoes ended up eating the bats! In 1982 the tower was added to the U.S. National Register of Historic Places and has become a popular backdrop for souvenir photos.

Photo by roboneal.com

Bigfoot the cat offers a steely stare.

MESSIN' WITH BIGFOOT

Only in Key West could the ownership rights to a 'Hemingway cat' end up as a messy courtroom drama. The gods must be crazy . . . .

Anyone familiar with the Keys will tell you there are some crime stories so loony they could only have happened here: Japanese exchange students caught red-handed photographing each other urinating on a police cruiser; a chihuahua accused of impregnating a neighbor's rottweiler; a man robbing a bank armed only with a plastic pitchfork. That kind of thing.

Most of these cases are strictly local curiosities, that generate convulsive laughter when they're broken in the *Key West Citizen* or, as so often happens, in *Key West The Newspaper*, an irreverent, free, weekly publication referred to by locals as the *"Blue Paper,"* that became an online-only news source in 2012.

Once in a while, though, our local press picks up on a story so unusual it transcends local folklore and becomes a genuine news item reported on by both the regional and national media in bewildered – perhaps morbid – fascination.

The following tale, involving the shockingly expensive legal tug-of-war over an aging, many-toed cat, is one such instance. But this is also a story of the tension between rich newcomers and the less well-heeled, working-class that's existed since Key West first embraced tourism during the Great Depression. Yes, even in this mellow island paradise the haves and have-nots butt heads from time to time.

* * *

One evening in early May of 2004 wealthy Truman Annex residents Joan and Tom Tukey were walking home toward their palatial Front Street mansion when a large orange-and-white cat with 15 toes on its front paws began following them. The critter-loving couple, convinced that the friendly feline was feral, rolled out their welcome mat, set out a dish of food – and then closed the front door behind the cat. Before long, they were calling their hungry houseguest "Toes," and discussing what to do with him.

At the same time, just a few blocks away, jewelry sales clerk Kathy Eddins was getting worried about her "Bigfoot." The plump, 11-year-old cat she had adopted from the Virginia Beach S.P.C.A. shelter as a kitten in 1993 hadn't returned home to spend the night on the foot of her bed as he usually did. Knowing that her pet was prone to wander, Eddins decided to give him until morning to show up, and then go out looking.

The next day, with Bigfoot still missing, Eddins put together "lost cat" posters and went door-to-door to see if any of her neighbors had seen him. She even inquired at the security guard post at the Southard Street entrance to the Annex, to no avail.

Little did this warm, yet tenacious breast cancer survivor know the legal and personal drama that lay ahead of her.

* * *

For many Key Westers, nothing epitomizes the island's social and economic divide like the Truman Annex. This gated waterfront community of high-end homes was built on land the U.S. Navy acquired in 1823 and later expanded to include annexed parts of the neighboring community now known as Bahama Village. Up until 1974 it was the southernmost naval base in the country. It was also home to President Harry S. Truman's "Winter White House," during the 11 working vacations he took here.

By the early 1970s, however, the base had become obsolete and the Navy decided to return it to the city – provided it was used for the benefit of all Key Westers. Before long, the parcel had been snapped up by aspiring real estate developer Pritam Singh and turned into luxury residences, complete with a homeowners association that by 2004 counted Tom Tukey as its president.

A smaller, far less exclusive component of the project called the Shipyard Condos was set aside as the "affordable housing" required by city law. It was into one of these modest, semi-detached units that Piedmont, California native Kathy Eddins moved, with her polydactyl* cat Bigfoot, in 1996.

* * *

In the days following Bigfoot's disappearance, on or around May 10, 2004, Eddins spent her time searching in vain for her precious pet, while Joan Tukey was out making similar inquiries in the neighborhood regarding her new furry friend "Toes." Like Eddins before her, Tukey also asked about the cat at the Southard Street security post, and later claimed that the guard there could give her no information.

For whatever reason, the two women missed running into each

---

*A polydactyl cat is an inbred specimen with more than five toes per front paw, a common sight in Key West. Despite claims that Ernest Hemingway brought six-toed cats to Key West from Cuba he never actually owned a single cat of any kind during the eight years he lived at 907 Whitehead St.

other during their respective searches like ships that pass in the night. Tukey later claimed that she also put out feelers to a number of local animal organizations, including the Key West S.P.C.A., to try to track down the pudgy puss's owner.

Though the exact chronology of events is still in dispute, it's clear that in the days following Bigfoot's disappearance from Eddins' life, Joan Tukey took "Toes" to the Lower Keys Animal Clinic for a checkup. It was there that she convinced a receptionist to adopt the animal. When the woman's other pets and "Toes" didn't get along, however, the feline was returned to Joan and Tom Tukey, who were at this point packing for a road trip up to their summer home in Bar Harbor, Maine. The couple was now unsure of what to do with "Toes," whom the veterinarian had informed her was missing his front claws but was otherwise healthy, so Joan Tukey bundled the 19-pound cat into the couple's car, and they set out on their trip up the Eastern Seaboard.

At some point along the way, the Tukeys received a call informing them that "Toes" did indeed have an owner, who was trying to locate her pet. The couple, and their bewildered passenger continued on to Maine regardless.

Around this time events got weird.

On the afternoon of Friday June 4 faithful readers of the *Blue Paper* were treated to the first, farcical details of this intensifying cat-fight. The tabloid's former publisher, Dennis Reeves Cooper, wasn't shy about covering the sensational developing stories that appeal to his readership, and the Bigfoot brief was no exception.

"Depending on whom you talk to, the Tukeys either rescued Bigfoot from a sad life of neglect – or they simply catnapped him and hauled him up to their summer home in Bar Harbor", Cooper wrote. "To make her point, [Eddins] has filed a report with the Key West Police Department."

This latter action irked the Tukeys who now claimed that Eddins was guilty of "inhumane animal neglect" for allowing her dirty, un-derfed, and declawed puss, to wander the neighborhood.

"[Our lawyer] will work to reach an agreement with her for the fair value of her lost property," Joan Tukey wrote imperiously in a May 31 statement. "If she does not want to come to an agreement

promptly and reasonably, then she should expect that we will immediately initiate several civil lawsuits against her. We will actively
and immediately pursue criminal charges against her for animal
cruelty according to Florida statutes. We will report her for the criminal charges of filing false police reports against us."

Eddins was blown away by the Tukeys' actions.

"Let me get this straight," she said. "They took my cat and they
want to sue *me*?"

Do as we say and all will be ok

the foundation must obtain Fifty Dollars by next meeting

at tHe tIMe OF tHe cRIMe...

On Tuesday, May 28, 2002, the Alice Foundation drinking/social club had its
mascot, a stuffed primate named "Alice" stolen, during a club meeting at the
Green Parrot Bar. Before long the kidnappers had made contact with several of
the group's members by both email and snail-mail, demanding that a donation
of $50 be made to the Florida Keys S.P.C.A. in exchange for Alice's "safe" return.
One letter contained a image of Alice made with a photocopier. Alice Foundation
member Leigh Pujado wrote about the episode in her column in the *Citizen's
Paradise This Week* section and promptly received an anonymous email sent
from an Internet café which read "I thought I said don't go to the press. Don't
make me hurt Alice – I am beginning to like the beast. You must follow my next
two commands. Strike one." Eventually the S.P.C.A. donation was paid and Alice
was returned unharmed.

The law seemed to be on the side of Eddins, who had wisely held onto Bigfoot's adoption papers.

"Under the law, an animal is property," said Florida Keys S.P.C.A. director Dean Humfleet, "and, apparently, Ms. Eddins has proof that she owns the cat. Therefore, even if the Tukeys assumed that the cat had been abused, neglected or abandoned, they had no legal right to just take it."

The situation was now bizarre.

By the time the July 30 *Blue Paper* hit the stands no fewer than four attorneys in two states were involved in the case. Eddins had retained lawyer Roberta Fine, while the Tukeys had snapped up legal eagle Jerry Coleman in Key West and an unnamed barrister in Bar Harbor. Key West jurist Ed Scales was set to act as a mediator at a scheduled session the next week.

"Our position is that once the Tukeys knew that Bigfoot had an owner and refused to return him, they committed theft," Fine said.

At this point Eddins had filed complaints with the Bar Harbor and Key West police departments and with the state attorney in Key West.

"All I want is my cat back," Eddins maintained. She had even offered to fly to Maine at her own expense to bring Bigfoot home, but claimed that the Tukeys had ignored her offer. The couple also apparently had launched a smear campaign against Eddins, claiming that certain unnamed Truman Annex residents were ready to testify that Bigfoot "seemed neglected," according to the *Blue Paper*.

Around this time, the Ellsworth, Maine weekly newspaper the *American* was calling Dennis Cooper for details and a photo. As Bigfoot/"Toes" languished in luxury in Bar Harbor the cat-spat had gone national.

The Oct. 8 *Blue Paper* revealed yet more ugliness. Even as Monroe County Judge Wayne Miller prepared to hear the case in small claims court, the Tukeys were now suing Eddins for defamation – for publicly accusing them of stealing her cat. The couple also claimed they had convinced the Virginia Beach S.P.C.A. to rescind Eddins' ownership of Bigfoot and transfer it to them, on the grounds that declawing the animal and allowing it to roam outside violated Eddins' adoption contract. The lawyers' fees were piling up on both sides.

Bizarre had become insane.

By late October, with revelers massing in Key West for the annual Fantasy Fest celebrations, Bigfoot/"Toes", by now the city's most famous cat, rolled back into town in the back seat of the Tukeys' car to preside over the craziness like an oversized float in the wacky parade.

Dennis Cooper seemed to realize he'd sunk his claws into a story with furry legs. Though the *Blue Paper's* coverage had been largely sympathetic to Eddins, the editor allowed the Tukeys space in the Nov. 26 and Dec. 3 editions to make their case.

The two self-serving guest columns stressed the "really filthy" condition "Toes" was in when he wandered up to them, and the cruelty Eddins displayed in having the cat declawed, (an action Eddins later testified was necessary to permit the over-toed cat to be able to walk properly.)

Moreover, while the Tukeys admitted their actions might seem "crazy" to some, they had been "SHOCKED" to learn that the Key West Police were investigating them for catnapping. Lastly, they implied that Eddins had used the whole affair to attempt to extort money from them. It had all led to their summer starting off on a "sour note," to "sleepless nights and much anxiety." People accosted them on the streets, over the phone and via email. Bags of cat crap had even been thrown at their Key West house. None of this had altered their convictions, though. The Tukeys steadfastly maintained that "animals are more than mere property," and that what they had done was right for "Toes" – and for all cats. "Treating animals as mere property is backward and ignorant," Tom Tukey wrote in a Nov. 2 statement. Just over two months later he would describe "Toes" as the couple's "rightful possession" in the *Washington Post*.

On Dec. 5, Jennifer Babson of the *Miami Herald* waded into the fray with a piece rife with "class warfare" overtones.

"Right now 'Toes' is living in the lap of luxury," she wrote. "He stretches on a mahogany coffee table, munches on tuna and chicken-flavored treats and dines on diabetic pet food from a sculpted brass food holder. Lately, his favorite activity seems to be lolling about the Tukeys' six-bedroom home, doing his business in a 3-foot-long litter box that rests in a bathroom off their Asian-inspired master bedroom."

As December progressed, the Tukeys went on the offensive, posting a $10,000 bond to retain possession of "Toes" until the trial was over.

They also had their new lawyer Cara Higgins threaten local animal rights advocate Nancy Fleming and her group "Friends of Bigfoot" with legal action should they refuse to cease running pro-Eddins advertisements in the *Blue Paper.*

The Dec. 17 issue also revealed that at one point Tom Tukey had become so vexed by the thought of his wife being arrested for theft that he entreated board members of the Truman Annex Master Property Owners Association to lobby State Attorney Mark Kohl on the couple's behalf.

At any rate it was all a moot point now. "Ms. Eddins no longer owns the cat," Tom Tukey said.

In a sworn deposition Eddins fired back, calling the Tukeys' charges of neglect a "smokescreen," and claiming that the Tukeys' former lawyer Jerry Coleman had offered her $10,000 for Bigfoot, which she refused. Her veterinarian Dr. Rex Cross stated "If I ever come back as an animal, I want to be Kathy Eddins' cat." In a sworn deposition a month later Cross elaborated, "This was a well-loved, well cared for cat."

By now it was clear that the Tukeys' PR offensive was bombing like Dukakis in '84. Even Dennis Cooper was fed up.

"Message to the Tukeys: Return the damn cat!" screamed the Dec. 31 *Blue Paper* headline.

In that issue Cooper called the entire case "ridiculous" and berated the Tukeys' litigious behavior which he said now even extended to threats against his own newspaper. "Might the phrase 'spoiled rich people' apply here?" Cooper wondered. "It is likely that whatever position they once held in high society here is rapidly going down the toilet."

On Jan. 2, *Washington Post* reporter Manuel Roig-Franzia added his two-cents. "Alley cats have had tamer encounters than the weird kitty custody case consuming the courts in the through-the-looking-glass world of Key West, Florida."

● ● ●

Finally, on Jan. 21 Judge Miller began to hear testimony in the small claims court case of Kathleen Eddins vs. Joan Tukey, Thomas Tukey and Catkind, Inc., a non-profit organization the couple had formed. And none of it was good news for the Tukeys. First, Chief Assistant State Attorney Jeff Overby revealed the Tukeys had called him from Maine and admitted they had no plans to return Bigfoot to Eddins. (He responded that they were breaking the law. They countered that he was "ignorant" and "uninformed.") They had also leaned on Overby to try to convince his boss not to pursue the matter in criminal court. (By now, the state attorney's office had opened a criminal investigation anyway.)

Next, a Key West S.P.C.A. employee put the lie to Joan Tukey's claim that she had alerted the organization to the found feline. (As it turned out, a friend of the Tukeys had called the S.P.C.A. on their behalf, but called back later to say the cat's owner had been located.)

The S.P.C.A. employee did confirm that Eddins' had reported her cat missing. "Had the Tukeys filed a found-cat report with the S.P.C.A., the shelter could have immediately told me where Bigfoot was," Eddins said.

More troubling testimony came from the guard on duty at the Southard Street security post, who recalled Joan Tukey's inquiry about Bigfoot on that fateful May evening. "I told her that such a cat did often visit the guard booth and I felt sure that he lived with someone who lives in Truman Annex – although I didn't know the name of the owner," the guard stated.

At long last, on Thursday, Feb. 10, came the ruling that everyone was expecting – except possibly the Tukeys: return the damn cat.

"The nature of this case is best explained in a Mark Twain quote," Miller noted wryly in his final judgment. "'I find that principles are not that important unless one is well fed.'"

Still, though the court had given the couple 72 hours to return Bigfoot to Eddins, the Tukeys had dodged a major bullet in that they were found guilty only of "conversion" of Eddins' property and not of civil theft, which would have obliged them to pay their rival's court costs, and possibly damages. Naturally the couple's lawyer asked Judge Miller to reconsider his ultimate ruling.

"We will comply with all court orders, period, end of story," Tom

Tukey told the *Citizen* after the trial. "Everybody thinks we're certifiable for spending tens of thousands of dollars on this issue . . . Cats and dogs aren't exactly kids, but they're not bicycles, either. They're living, feeling things and it's not right that they're not cared for."

Eddins' lawyer Roberta Fine was of three minds regarding the verdict: pleased that Eddins got her cat back; disappointed that court costs were not awarded; baffled that the case had actually taken place at all.

"I don't think, in my 22-year career, I have ever had this many depositions in a small claims case," she said. "The court reporter fees have been astronomical. This is one of those 'only in Key West' things."

• • •

Epilogue:
Two days after the trial, Tom Tukey sent Eddins an email, part carrot, part stick, to convince her to leave Bigfoot with them. "We could work out an agreement which would never have to be disclosed to anyone," Tukey wrote. Should Eddins relinquish ownership, the Tukeys might help her "work it out" with her lawyer's fees, and allow her to visit the feline from time to time. Should she refuse to do so, however, she could expect a lawsuit from the Virginia Beach S.P.C.A. that they would "likely eventually win." Eddins ignored the email. Shortly afterwards, Bigfoot was returned to Eddins, 5 pounds heavier, but otherwise unruffled by the whole experience. Sadly, but wisely, Eddins concluded that Bigfoot's roaming days were over and she bought a leash with which to walk him.

A few days later Eddins received a certified letter from the Virginia Beach S.P.C.A. ordering her to drop Bigfoot off at the Tukeys' lawyers' office or face a lawsuit. Eddins refused. Nothing happened. On Feb. 11, Judge Miller decided that the Tukeys should pay Eddins' court costs after all.

The cat and mouse game was finally over.

Nearly seven years, and over $100,000 in court fees later, Bigfoot died on Dec. 29, 2010 with Eddins at his side.

"He had a long and full life," she said.

As for the Tukeys, not long after the resolution of the case, they fulfilled Dennis Cooper's prophecy regarding their future social status here: they left Key West with their tails between their legs.

"THE ST. TROPEZ OF THE POOR"

Though onetime Key West resident Ernest Hemingway was reportedly an anti-New Deal Republican, he was sympathetic to the plight of the destitute of Key West, which he described as "The St. Tropez of the poor."

In *To Have and Have Not*, (1939,) he scripted this exchange between two of its main characters:

"'What they're trying to do is starve you Conchs out of here so they can burn down the shacks and put up apartments and make this a tourist town. That's what I hear. I hear they're buying up lots, and then after the poor people are starved out and gone somewhere else to starve some more they're going to come in and make it into a beauty spot for tourists."

"'You talk like a radical,' I said."

Google maps

THE BIG PINE 29

*In the early 1980s lawmen tried to stamp
out marijuana smuggling in Monroe County.
A spectacular bust in the Middle Keys revealed
the true scope of the problem . . .*

B y now, anyone with a passing familiarity with the Keys knows something of the history of pot smuggling here. Briefly, it began in the early 1970s, became a staple industry by the end of the decade, and flamed out in the late '80s due to increased police effort and changes in the drug business itself.

Nowadays, the high-potency, hydroponic herb American smokers buy likely originated in Canada, California, or possibly even at a small grow-op in the Keys. Back in the 1970s through mid-'80s though, the trade routes usually brought "flexi-Mexi" Colombian grass to the States by way of boat docks and fishing ports in places like South Florida.

Isolated and corrupt, the Keys were a natural unloading zone. Waterfront estates located far off the beaten path became known as "smuggler's specials" and served as perfect places to get the job done.

Nelson 'Ping Ping' Jamardo in 1980.

It was at just such a dockside retreat that a legendary Keys pot bust took place, snaring a mind-boggling number of local smugglers in its legal net.

• • •

It began, as is so often the case, with a tip-off to the cops.

In October of 1980, both U.S. Customs Agent Greg V. Welch, and the Monroe County Sheriff's Office received information that someone was using the area around the Cohen Estate on Warner Street, Big Pine Key, as a marijuana offloading site. The agencies believed the information to be credible, and along with the Florida Marine Patrol, set up sporadic surveillance of the island.

Viewed from the air, this exclusive gated property on the bayside of Big Pine Key at first seems like the perfect spot for a pot drop. It's located on a dead-end street and surrounded by woods, water and wire fences, and the lot and its dock are located on an inland canal far from the prying eyes of neighbors. It still had easy access to both Florida Bay and the Atlantic.

The location's Achilles heel, in hindsight, may have been that it was just a bit too close to U.S. Highway 1 and the bridges that carry that road north towards Marathon. It was from these vantage points that the authorities were able to monitor the comings and goings at the estate's canal.

About a month into the investigation, on the cold and rainy afternoon of Nov. 14, Monroe County Sheriff's Detectives Mike Barber and Steve Coletti were stationed at a surveillance point on the Seven Mile Bridge, when they observed two small "T-craft" boats pass beneath them, heading north. One of the boats veered west towards Big Pine Key and as the detectives followed U.S. 1 south to the north end of the Spanish Harbor Bridge, the craft and its single occupant entered the canal leading to the Cohen Estate. At this point Agent Welch joined Coletti. Not long afterward the pair observed the same vessel leaving the canal, this time loaded down with six or seven people. The craft headed towards Marathon, then abruptly turned north into the Gulf of Mexico. This was a major red flag, and full surveillance of the Cohen Estate by land and sea began in earnest.

As darkness fell and heavy rain poured down, two officers manned the Spanish Harbor Bridge stakeout while two others patrolled the bayside of Big Pine.

Down the road from the estate Welch, Coletti and Barber navigated thick mangrove swamp as they slowly and stealthily made their way toward the Cohen property, stalking their quarry like famished Florida panthers.

The agents secreted themselves in bushes across from the padlocked gate, where they watched and waited. After a while a man appeared out of the gloom, walking towards the gate. He spied the three lawmen and called out to them in Spanish. The cops, fearing that their cover had been blown, quickly snatched the man and

at tHe tI Me Of tHe cRI Me...

On March 1, 1980, Key West Police Sgt. Harry Lariz Jr. was viciously attacked while responding to a domestic dispute call on Galveston Lane. William E. Smith was charged with attempted murder of a police officer as a result.

whisked him from the site.

"Ah, mi madre, the police," the startled smuggler cried as he was carted off, according to the Nov. 15 *Key West Citizen.*

Next, the three officers made their way to the edge of the Spanish Harbor Channel to keep an eye on the entrance to the canal with a high-powered nightscope, occasionally wading out into the water for a better look. Around 2 a.m. on Nov. 15 they heard a boat enter the canal and cut its engine. Welch would later describe the sound he heard next as "thuds, a hollow thudding." A short time later Welch watched another boat navigate into the canal and heard the same thudding sound. Convinced they were literally hearing bales of grass hit the dock at Cohens, the trio returned to the bushes near the front gate to plot their next move.

Welch then walked across U.S.1 to a rock quarry where his commanding officer Major Monty Seals was waiting. They lacked a search warrant but decided to hop the fence anyway. After issuing orders to cut off all avenues of escape, Seals, Welch and two other officers made their way to the Cohen gate where they met up with Coletti and Barber. By 3:30 a.m. the six cops were over the wall and walking down the muddy dirt road in the direction of the main building on the property, passing a parked white van along the way.

As they approached the house the strong smell of pot wafted through the drenching rain. Through the darkness three men emerged from the building's garage and were quickly busted. A fourth man ran from the house toward the waterfront. Detective Barber chased this suspect for 100 yards or so before firing a couple of warning shots in the air. The perp tripped and finally surrendered. Barber restrained the man and began walking him back to the main building, where the bust was now in full swing.

The lawmen had just entered the house, announcing their presence over blaring rock music to a gaggle of men gathered in the living room, when Welch rounded a corner of the house with another suspect in tow. The officer quickly discovered another suspect sitting on a rock wall near the garage and arrested him too. In the garage Welch noted a busted-into bale – patched with a Colombian newspaper – and some smaller packages of weed strewn on the floor.

On the east side of the house Patrolman Leonard noticed a large, white delivery van and looked underneath. This move yielded another suspect, who was marched inside with the others. Returning to the van, Leonard found yet another man stuck in the bushes nearby and escorted him into the living room as well.

Around this time, Detective Barber and his collar arrived back at the house. Over the din of the downpour, Barber could hear an approaching boat and notified his colleagues that more dopers were on their way.

The cops made their way to the dock and hid their faces, just in time to catch the bowlines thrown to them by the smugglers' T-craft. The four men in the boat were popped for the 83 bales they had on board, then cuffed, and hustled off to the Cohen house. The arrests were adding up, but the night was young. While securing the crime scene Seals heard movement overhead. A trap-door in the garage bathroom revealed an attic crawlspace and another five suspects were added to the evening's haul.

Out on the water, the Marine Patrol had stopped another T-craft for "proceeding without running lights," adding four more arrestees to the rolls. Finally the cops discovered the mothership itself, a 40-foot lobster fishing boat, the *Miss Lucy*, out of Marathon, idling in the channel. Two more would-be smugglers were taken into custody, for a grand total of 30 arrests in all. This number was a record for a single Florida Keys bust, and one of the largest ever in the state of Florida. The cops had seized 31,000 pounds of the drug, not counting the loads of residue scattered across the floors of the house. The street value was said to be a cool $2 million in 1980 dollars. Also seized were the two T-crafts, the *Miss Lucy*, a gold-painted Cadillac, a pickup truck, a van, and two larger trucks emblazoned with the Sears department store logo. A smattering of high-end weaponry was also nabbed, including pearl handled automatic pistols – and even a miniature replica of an old Colt 45.

● ● ●

As can be imagined, the fallout from such a huge federal operation was overwhelming to the Keys small-town legal system.

"Where the hell am I going to put them?" Sheriff Billy Freeman Jr. wondered aloud to the *Citizen*. "The Holiday Inn doesn't check as many people in and out a day as I do." Late on Nov. 15, bleary-eyed relatives arrived at the Whitehead Street sheriff's office to bond out their busted loved ones, and details began to emerge about the individuals involved in the smuggling ring. In contrast to many previous cases, a number of these smugglers were locals with familiar names.

The Key West-based notables included David Electric owner Antonio Hernandez; Sears salesman Manuel Sanchez; former Navy fireman Francisco Hernandez; and dePoo Hospital nurse Domingo F. Galvan, and his brother Sergio Galvan, whom Domingo had brought over from Cuba during the Mariel Boatlift, less than a year earlier.

Other, lesser-known figures hailed from Stock Island, Big Pine, Marathon, and Dade County on the mainland. A lone individual, Norman Lee Young, gave a Hilton Head, South Carolina address. Young's involvement led authorities to speculate that the Palmetto State may have been the ultimate destination for the drugs.

The best-known of all the detainees, though, was well-known fisherman, boat mechanic and car dealership co-owner Nelson "Ping Ping" Jamardo, of Geiger Key. During the upcoming trial, the U.S. Army veteran's name would figure prominently among the defendants, as suspicion centered upon him as the alleged ringleader.

The drama intensified at the sheriff's office when "a reporter for the *Miami Herald* who wanted to take pictures of the arrested men was threatened by the lobby crowd, who warned him that neither he nor the camera would make it out of the building unharmed if he took the photos," the *Citizen* reported. "He didn't." (Outside the courthouse however, the angry mob did knock *Herald* photog Robert Rivas to the ground, smashed his camera, and destroyed the film inside. Nelson Jamardo was charged with criminal mischief and assault in the incident but was cleared on May 10, 1981.)

● ● ●

At this point a brief aside on "Ping Ping" might be in order.

Key West native Nelson Jamardo had gone to work for Charley Toppino & Sons at the age of 15. Over the course of his life he watched as his hometown became more and more expensive to live in. By the mid-1970s Jamardo's salary was stuck at about $16,000 per year, and it was getting tougher to feed his family. As the American economic "malaise" wore on into the late '70s Jamardo, (nicknamed "Ping Ping" by his boss George Toppino for the hollow ring his rail-thin body would be likely to give off if flicked,) became a smuggler. So many of Jamardo's fellow fishermen had already taken to "the life," that it seemed like a no-brainer to him.

Of course this in itself eventually became a problem. Few people were actually being caught, and of those who were, the sentences meted out were remarkably light.

These actions gave "Ping Ping" and his colleagues a feeling of invincibility and they started to get sloppy. One day in the late '70s, the supposedly struggling shrimper walked into a Mercedes dealership in Miami and paid cash for three brand new cars. The feds were duly notified and took note of the big-spending fisherman. "Ping Ping" then bought a piece of the Bevis-Lewis Chevy dealership in Key West, likely to use the operation as a money-laundering vehicle.

A close call came in 1979, when the feds boarded "Ping Ping's" shrimp boat *The Selena* and discovered 33 tons of reefer, but the captain was released without charges, adding to his sense of immunity. In reality he was now under constant surveillance by the authorities.

Thus, it was with no sense of dread whatsoever that the easygoing smuggler pulled up to the dock at the Cohen place that stormy November night and threw his mooring lines to Coletti and Barber.

● ● ●

In December 1980, a federal grand jury in Miami returned indictments against all but one of the accused. The smugglers were now collectively dubbed the "Big Pine 29" by the police and press, and were headed to court, all charged with "conspiracy to knowingly and intentionally posses with intent to distribute" marijuana. They were also charged with actual possession of marijuana, with intent to distribute it.

The trial promised to be messy. The sheer number of defendants and lawyers and their motions to suppress the massive physical evidence were stacking up even before the jury had been selected.

The defense team, led by local heavyweights Alvin Entin, Mitchell Denker, and Nathan Eden, was formidable.

In a nutshell, all of the accused asserted that their rights had been violated during the bust. Attorneys for the six men arrested aboard the *Miss Lucy* and the T-craft without lights maintained that there had been no probable cause to stop them or link them to the pinch taking place at the Cohen Estate. Counselors for the other 23 similarly claimed that given the lack of a search warrant, the arresting officers had no right to enter the Cohen property.

In Miami, Federal Magistrate Herbert Shapiro had earlier recommended suppressing the evidence against the six but not the 23. Accordingly the prosecution appealed the decision regarding the six while the defense appealed the finding on the 23.

At the Key West trial U.S. District Court Judge James Lawrence King ultimately gave the prosecution, led by Assistant U.S. Attorney Leah Simms, exactly what they wanted. The evidence against all 29 would be admitted, under promise of appeal by the nine defense lawyers.

Thus the court action, which began on Feb. 2 in King's courtroom at the federal building on Simonton Street, lived up to its billing by the *Citizen* as a "trial of motions." Unfortunately for the "29," defense attorneys seemed to be losing them all. Over the next four weeks the nine lawyers objected to allowing the arresting officers to sit at the prosecution table, reminded the jury that it was "not the obligation of the defendants to prove anything," described the bust as a "general dragnet on Big Pine Key," and accused the government of "butchering" the chain of evidence. (One customs officer testified that he brought three times as much Big Pine pot to the Miami incinerator as had actually been confiscated at the Cohen place.) The defense demanded a mistrial after the prosecution introduced evidence that hadn't been outlined to them, and they complained that a customs agent had eavesdropped on their conversations with their clients in the courthouse hallways.

Aggravated by these distractions, Judge King threatened to grant the mistrial motion, but allowed the trial to continue regardless. The controversy did claim one victim: Leah Simms was edged out as lead prosecutor by her colleague Assistant U.S. Attorney Tom Sclafani.

41

By the time the final defense witness was called on Feb. 25, the "29" had been reduced to "26" following the acquittal of the two men aboard the *Miss Lucy*, and the severance of another man from the main group of defendants.

Attorney Alvin Entin marked the end of the historic trial by presenting Judge King with a bright yellow shirt emblazoned with the words "Big Pine 29 – Judge."

This levity on the part of the defense was short-lived. On Feb. 28 the jury convicted all 22 of the men who had been captured at the Cohen Estate, acquitting only the four stopped in the unlighted T-craft in the Spanish Harbor Channel.

The scene was an emotional one that saw Judge King seal the courtroom doors and had one defense lawyer repeating the word "bizarre" several times. A prosecutor said he had "never seen anything like the situation in his years on the job." Yet another declared "I want to see the movie."

In an unusual move both defense and prosecution had agreed to accept a less than unanimous verdict rather than see what had been a hung jury force a new trial. "I've never heard of it before and I've been a judge 10 years," King later told the *Citizen*. "I've never known a jury to do this. This may be the first time . . . in this country."

In essence, both sides had rolled the dice. The defense had crapped out.

All of the convicted were to remain free on bond pending sentencing, but higher bail was now demanded of six smugglers. Francisco Hernandez and Raul Hernandez were obliged to post personal surety bonds of $150,000, while $250,000 was demanded of Nelson "Ping Ping" Jamardo, Richard Mungin, Norman L. Young, and Antonio Hernandez.

The penalty phase began on April 20 and resulted in "eight of the stiffest sentences ever given to smugglers in the Keys – five to 15 years," according to the *Citizen*. Several days later Judge King broke his own records when he handed an 18-year bid and $250,000 fine to Norman Lee Young of Hilton Head – said by the feds to have been involved in other large-scale smuggling operations – and an 18-year term and $50,000 levy to Richard Mungin of Stock Island.

The final defendant, "Ping Ping" Jamardo, was granted a delay to line up witnesses to counter prosecution claims that he was a "major narcotics smuggler" with numerous other alleged offences to his name. It didn't help that the *Miami Herald* was running stories about his extravagant lifestyle, however. According to one report, Jamardo's home was "equipped with sophisticated parabolic microphones to detect intruders. His investments include automobiles and boats, houses and land. He reports a modest income far exceeded by huge expenditures of cash."

Jamardo's lawyers were said to be in talks with Assistant U.S. Attorney Sclafani, but whatever deal they might have been hoping to strike seemed to fall by the wayside by May 12. On that date, King sentenced Jamardo to an eye-watering 21-year jail term and $250,000 fine. There was little doubt that both the judge and the government were sending a strong message to other would-be smugglers: attempt this at your own peril.

In April, 1983 a federal appeals court upheld all the convictions, and "Ping Ping" was off to the Big House.

• • •

By the end of the decade, the Wild West era of Keys pot-smuggling had passed and Jamardo, now 50, and with salt-and-pepper hair, had served a "hard nickel" and then some. On Jan. 24, 1989, he stood before Judge King once more – this time to petition the man who had thrown the book at him, for a sentence reduction.

To the surprise and delight of many, King sprang Jamardo that very day, to applause from the 15 or so of "Ping Ping's" friends and relatives in attendance. The reason, King explained, was assistance the smuggler had rendered the U.S. Attorney of the Northern District of Florida around the time of the original trial. Promises of consideration had been made to "Ping Ping" for his cooperation, but never relayed to the judge by the defense lawyers. This omission, King stated, had led to "traumatic" and "unjust" experience for the accused. In order to make it right, Jamardo would be set free.

The Florida Keys had changed greatly during Jamardo's time in the joint. In the 1980s tourism came to dominate the economy and high-profile new arrivals such as Calvin Klein and Roy Scheider had put prosperous Key West on the "it" destination map.

Jamardo rejoined the outside world not as a "major narcotics smuggler" but as a "trusted" and "capable" employee of Charley Toppino & Sons. By now, all his "Big Pine 29" cohorts have also been released. Some have become respectable family men; some are dead.

The Cohen Estate itself has been razed to make way for a larger and even more exclusive structure.

But the old-timers still recall that chaotic weekend in November of 1980 when the legendary pot-smuggling industry reached its zenith – on a windswept, waterfront estate on Big Pine Key . . .

SMUGGLER'S ISLAND

Hiaasen

In March of 1980 the *Miami Herald* sent three reporters to the Keys to investigate the growing problem of drugs in the island chain. The resulting newspaper stories were eventually reprinted in a special edition booklet titled *Key West – Smuggler's Island*. Among the intrepid scoops who contributed to the stories was famed Florida writer, and current *Herald* columnist, Carl Hiaasen.

THIS IS A REPRINT OF A MIAMI HERALD SERIES PUBLISHED FROM MARCH 16 TO MARCH 21, 1980

Courtesy of Monroe County Library

Joseph 'Bongo Billy' Giebel, during his trial.

'STREETS OF KEY WEST'

Tourist Sherri Lynn Jett had the misfortune of meeting up with the worst elements of Key West's underclass. It took an idealistic group of youthful nomads to help see justice done . . .

J ust as sun-drenched Southern California is a refuge from the cold for west coast drifters and indigents, so too is tropical Key West a mecca for their counterparts in the east. Lured by the balmy weather and relatively lax loitering laws, most of these individuals seek merely to live and let live. Still others harbor true hearts of darkness and depravity. Key West may be an intoxicant-fueled adult playground, but like all cities it has its seamy and dangerous side. The following is a cautionary tale of what can happen when a carefree vacationer wanders off the friendly and fun-loving main streets and takes a walk down the seedy, dark alleys where the devils meet.

● ● ●

His schedule was more or less the same every day.

Joseph Giebel, aka "Bongo Billy" would rise, shake the booze and drug cobwebs from his head, then go see what sort of labor his benefactor, Jabour's Trailer Court, required from him that day.

When his menial tasks were completed, Giebel would sit in the doorway of the William Street warehouse where Jabour's let him keep a ratty, makeshift apartment, and play the Haitian Tonton Macoutes death march on his bongo drums. Often Giebel's beatnik appearance and wharf rat patois attracted an audience. Sometimes these were gawking, camera-wielding tourists, or the supple, young "Rainbow Family" hippie girls Giebel coveted. More frequently, his visitors were like Giebel himself: sketchy, unemployed ex-cons, and the drug-addled hookers who clung to them like raffish remoras to a slew of shifty sharks.

Saturday, April 24, 1998 began much like any other day for the white-haired, 55-year-old handyman. Fate intervened to ensure it ended quite differently.

● ● ●

Not six blocks away – but a social world apart – Sherri Lynn Jett's day was off to a rocky start. The 41-year-old tourist and her fiancé Donald Wright, 44, of Jensen Beach, Florida. were arguing about Jett's out-of-control drinking. When she was sober, Wright later testified, Jett was a loving girlfriend and responsible small business owner. When she fell off the wagon, as she had the night before in Key West, all bets were off. Jett's "continuous fight with alcoholism" had been on full display at the last bar on their crawl, where she keeled over and fell. Drunk beyond words, Jett had resembled a "rag doll" during her stagger back to their hotel.

That Saturday morning, following their argument, Jett hit Wright up for money to go get some breakfast. Though he feared the cash was probably going to be used to launch another drinking binge,

Wright forked over $7 anyway. It was a decision he would live to regret.

"I love you Don," were Jett's last words as she kissed him goodbye. "I'll be back in a little bit." She wasn't. And as morning became afternoon Wright became concerned that his fiancée had run into trouble. He spent most of the day searching frantically for Jett at all her favorite bars, and even called her business partner back in Jensen Beach to see if she had checked in. She hadn't.

The next day, Wright continued his search. He also called the hospital emergency room, the jail, and finally – the police, to officially report Jett missing. But no trace of her could be found.

Early on Monday morning Wright made his way down to the Key West Bight, where the Schooner Wharf Bar's so-called "Breakfast Club" gets drinking at 7 a.m. A couple of hours later, he took a walk up William Street, past a run-down warehouse at the edge of the Jabour property. Next door, at the West Marine boating supply store, Wright's heart sank when he saw a police van and a crowd gathered around a dumpster sealed off with yellow crime scene tape.

"I got this gut reaction and said 'Oh, my God,'" he later testified.

Wright's instincts were spot-on. Not long afterwards he was advised by the authorities that he had indeed stumbled across the site where his bride-to-be had been found brutally beaten, sadistically assaulted and viciously murdered.

With Jett's body on the way to the medical examiner the Key West Police set about trying to figure out who in this small community could have committed such a perverted and horrific crime - and why.

● ● ●

To solve the mystery, the cops first needed to retrace Jett's steps from the time she bade farewell to Don Wright and hit the streets of Key West with $7 to her name.

As Wright suspected, Jett had indeed been drawn to the Schooner Wharf for an eye-opener, like an alcoholic moth to a neon beer sign. According to witnesses, she had then bounced around the Bight most of the day in the company of a man whose name was well-known to all in the neighborhood – William Nelson Kirby, aka "Bongo Billy," aka Joseph Giebel, and a half-dozen other aliases.

Detectives wasted no time issuing a BOLO alert for Kirby, who by now was nowhere to be found. On April 29, the *Key West Citizen* printed a photo of Kirby/Giebel along with an entreaty to call Key West Police with information. It was soon revealed to the officer that Giebel had once stated his intention to "blend in" with the Rainbow Family, should he ever run into trouble. This gave Det. Sgt. John Hardy an idea. After doing a little research online he discovered that the "Family," which promotes alternative, non-violent lifestyles and often visits Key West, was planning on gathering in early July in the mountains near Eagle, Arizona, in the northeastern part of that state. Hardy sent the group an email explaining the situation, and crossed his fingers. The move turned out to be a brilliant one on Hardy's part.

As Giebel sat playing his bongo drums in a lawn chair at the gathering, he was surrounded by members of the Family's security force, known as the Shantasena, and detained until the police came to arrest him. Some say he was tied to a tree when the cops arrived.

"I know I'll never be free again," the suspect confessed to Hardy on the way to the Albuquerque airport.

By May 4, Giebel was formerly charged with murder.

● ● ●

The horrifying circumstances surrounding Sherri Lynn Jett's agonizing death, and the already sketchy reputation of her accused killer had dealt Giebel's lawyer Julio Margalli a lousy hand. Desperately digging around for reasonable doubt, the public defender hoped he had found it in a report from Monroe County Medical Examiner's Office. According to the pronouncement, Jett had bled to death from a ruptured colon caused by the indelicate insertion of an 18-inch dildo into her lower extremities, which was discovered inside her body. Considering that her blood/alcohol level was nearly four times the legal limit, it was just possible, the report allowed, that Jett had sustained the mortal trauma during the course of rough, but consensual sex and that her alcohol-dulled senses had kept her from realizing the seriousness of her injury.

"In no way do I want to cast aspersions on this lady," Margalli told the *Citizen* on Feb. 10, 1999. "But she may have died in her sleep . . . [the report] throws a monkey wrench into the state's murder charge . . . we definitely don't feel it's a first-degree murder charge."

Left unexplained by Margalli were the vicious abrasions on Jett's back and head and her fractured collarbone. One law enforcement officer who had seen the body called the wounds "consistent with defensive injuries indicating the victim attempted to fight off this attack."

● ● ●

The trial began on May 17, 2000 in the Key West courtroom of Circuit Court Judge Richard Payne. A jury of seven men and five women would decide Giebel's fate.

By now Giebel had swapped out Margalli for co-counsels Jason Smith and Richard Wunsch, who continued to insist that Jett's death had been accidental. Wunsch even claimed to be providing his services pro bono, out of a conviction that his client was innocent. Representing the people were lead prosecutor Jon Ellsworth and his co-counsel, ironically named Sherri Lyn Collins.

During his opening statement Ellsworth provided a preview of forthcoming testimony from a state witness to Jett's day-long drinking binge that Saturday at the Bight. The witness had engaged in intimate contact with Jett himself that day and had seen Giebel in close proximity to the victim as she lay unconscious on the sidewalk, Ellsworth said. Jett and Giebel had been seen together by others that day as well, according to the prosecutor.

The defense opened by attacking Monroe County Medical

at tHe tI Me OF tHe cRI Me...

In December of 1999 authorities were investigating a bizarre murder involving multiple jurisdictions. Jerry "Jake" Hamlin confessed that he had literally hammered Jesse Childs to death as he slept in his West Isle Club apartment bed. Hamlin then drove to south Miami where he castrated and beheaded the body and tossed it in a canal. He drove Childs' sheet-wrapped head back to Key West, where it was found "deep in the mangroves" at Little Hamaca Park.

Examiner Richard O. Eicher, alleging he had resigned his previous ME post under pressure from the Pinellas-Pasco County "because of questions about 150 autopsies" he had taken part in. Attorney Wunsch also pointed out that Jett had engaged in sex acts with multiple partners that weekend, and that one of the state's witnesses was "a local prostitute" who had "even called the police later to tell them they were all wrong about any beating" of Jett by Giebel. The trial was off to an ugly start.

It got even worse the next day during testimony from prosecution witness James Gerow, one of several men who had been sitting in a work van near Geibel's doorway early that morning when Jett happened by. He claimed that she had asked the group for beer but had been given pot instead. By 9 a.m. she was passed out naked in the vehicle. It was then that Gerow engaged in a sexual act with the prostrate Jett. Gerow left but returned at 11 a.m. "with friends 'to see the naked woman,'" who by now was lying on the sidewalk. The witness said he picked her up and returned her to the van as Giebel sat in the front seat, playing his drums. At 1:30 p.m. Gerow returned a final time to find Jett still blacked out.

As Gerow described the indignities visited upon the victim that day, Jett's mother and aunt sat expressionless in the courtroom, having been warned by the prosecution that any emotional outbursts could be considered grounds for a mistrial – or even an acquittal.

However, Jett's fiancé Don Wright glared at Giebel twice during the proceedings, causing one attorney to quip "if looks could kill, we wouldn't need the electric chair."

Wright gave his account of his final moments with Jett but the most important witness of the day was probably one Leonidas Hindes, who admitted that he helped Giebel carry Jett's body to the dumpster where she was found. The noose was beginning to tighten around Giebel's neck.

● ● ●

On April 19, Key West Police Sergeant John Hardy related to a hushed courtroom what Giebel had told him following his arrest in Arizona.

"He said 'I know what you're here for and I want to talk to you because I did not kill that woman.' When I asked him if he knew his Miranda rights he replied, 'Better than you do.'"

Eventually, Hardy testified, Giebel admitted that he was responsible for Jett's death, and had been planning to disappear into the backwoods of Alaska.

As to the details of Jett's death, Giebel told Hardy he had encountered the drunk and half-naked Jett in the van outside his residence and thought she was a prostitute. The vehicle's owner had offered him the use of the van – and Jett – for $20. Giebel said he refused the deal and instead had brought the inebriated woman back to his place where they engaged in "normal . . . tender . . . loving sex." During the course of their relations there had been some confusion about sex toys they were using, though, and when he left to grab a six-pack, he returned to find Jett passed out on his couch.

At this point, Giebel said a local "crack whore" he knew showed up at his door and shortly alerted him that she thought Jett was dead. Another Giebel acquaintance stopped by and after discussing the situation over lunch at the nearby VFW post, helped him dump Jett's body next door at West Marine. Giebel then hitchhiked out of town.

Sgt. Hardy had been the first officer on the scene at Giebel's apartment and described the couch in question as looking like a "bloody sponge," pieces of which were shown to the jury. Giebel's explanation for Jett's death was, Hardy told the court, "ludicrous."

The prosecution rested.

The next day, the court began hearing testimony from defense witnesses, including one deemed so unreliable that her deposition had been videotaped beforehand in case she didn't show up to court – which she didn't. Thirty-year-old "hooker with a heart of gold" Regina "Jeannie" Smale said she stopped by Giebel's lair for a beer around 6:30 a.m. on Sunday, April 25. He had been asleep and Smale had noticed a woman face-down and motionless on the floor.

"She was lying on her side, on her hands and looked like she was sleeping," Smale said. "If you got something going on, I'll leave," she told Giebel. As she headed for the door, she stopped to take the woman's pulse and found none. The stranger's face was blue.

"Jesus, Billy, she ain't passed out, she's dead," Smale said as she flew out of the building.

Another witness, Michele Sands, had been sitting at the Schooner Wharf that Saturday and told the court she saw Jett at the bar between 11 p.m. and midnight.

"She had no shoes on," Sands said. "Her feet were dirty. She walked past and smiled at me and I smiled back at her."

Jett then left Schooners – with Giebel.

On April 25, two years to the day that Sherri Lynn Jett's body was stuffed in the dumpster, the final defense witness was called. Miami rectal surgeon Dr. Michael Hellinger described various objects he had removed from patients, including "perfume and shampoo bottles, different fruits and a baseball with tacks," and scoffed at the idea that the death dildo could have been inserted without Jett's cooperation.

As the trial wound down many observers felt the case against Giebel was far from a slam dunk, a feeling that was reflected in a courtroom outburst by the accused.

"Kill me or let me go home," he stated aloud. "I didn't do nothing."

In the end both these options were rejected.

On April 26, 2000, the jury found Giebel guilty of first-degree murder and sexual battery with a weapon. Three weeks later, the same jury recommended permanent incarceration for the twice-married father of four. Judge Payne made it official on June 25.

"Miss Jett was a fellow human being, a caring and loving human being," Payne told Giebel. "She had the misfortune of encountering you, a convicted sexual batterer. This court . . . sentences you to life in prison without possibility of parole."

The convicted murderer showed no emotion as the sentence was passed.

"I'll save my breath in this court," he said. "I'll do my talking in an appellate court . . . I just want to get the hell out of here so I can go smoke a cigarette."

● ● ●

Unfortunately for Giebel, the jury's verdict was definitive. The psycho handyman/wannabe bongo drummer lost his appeals, and on July 21, 2000, was moved to his new home, the South Florida Reception Center South, in suburban Miami.

The building in which the brutal murder took place has been torn down for some years now, its heinous past gradually erased from memory, like a Polaroid in reverse. But the memory of Joseph "Bongo Billy" Giebel lingers as a stark warning to future Sherri Lynn Jetts:

Come to Key West. Enjoy our beaches and bars. But keep your wits about you. Don't overdo it on the party favors.

Above all, as Hill Street Blues Sgt. Phil Esterhaus used to say every day, "let's be careful out there!"

PAVING OVER THE PAIN

The area where Sherri Lynn Jett was brutalized and murdered has been undergoing a renaissance of late, with a hotel development planned for the former site of Jabour's, and upscale new shops and restaurants scheduled to open in the surrounding area.

This house at 1016 Howe St. in Bahama Village was once Key West's premier brothel.

THE HOUSE
ON HOWE STREET

Key West's Red Light District was a testament to the town's tolerance. A mysterious killing changed that forever . . .

Key West's buildings hide their secrets well.

In some parts of America, structures with notorious pasts are turned into tourist attractions, such as the Fall River, Massachusetts home of Lizzie Borden and her family – now a bed-and-breakfast and true crime buff destination. Elsewhere, such edifices are simply leveled, like the suburban Chicago home of mass murderer John Wayne Gacy or the Milwaukee apartment building of serial killer

Jeffrey Dahmer.

In the Southernmost City, though, buildable land is so scarce and Old Town historic preservation codes so strict that crime scenes are usually reincarnated as fashionable homes and businesses, betraying no inkling of the horrors that transpired within.

One such structure is the bright yellow gingerbread house at 1016 Howe St. in Bahama Village.

● ● ●

Prostitution is often described as "the world's oldest profession," and it naturally sprang up during Key West's earliest days. Beginning in the 1820s, the trade flourished in the gritty saloons that lined the booming waterfront.

As this international port grew in both size and importance, more "houses of ill fame," as they were referred to in the local press, opened, mainly in the area now known as Bahama Village.

The trains of Henry Flagler's Florida East Coast Railway began bringing carloads of tourists to Key West in 1912. By the time of Prohibition, many of these travelers arrived eager to sample the town's illicit pleasures, especially since bootleg booze from Cuba and The Bahamas continued to flow freely here during the 1920s and early '30s.

Among the favorite fleshpots in the pre-World War II era were The Square Roof, at the corner of Emma and Petronia streets; Florine's, at Fort and Petronia; and Big Annie's, located on Center Street, between Front and Greene streets.

The best-known bordello of them all, though, was the Howe Street house run by Alice Reid and her husband Marvin Griffin.

The house and bar, noted for its well-kept interior and hospitable "Georgia peach" girls, stood out from its neighbors by the traditional red light on the front porch. Nightly, this beacon was extinguished in time for "last call," wrote the late *Key West Citizen* reporter and columnist Dorothy Raymer in her 1981 book *Key West Collection*.

"Rules were strictly kept and the house closed bar and bed business promptly at 2 a.m. The owner supervised the shuttering and kept order. All was well and the routine adhered to, except for one person."

This individual was a Key West taxi driver named Graydon Plowman who, according to Raymer, kept a regular 3 a.m. rendezvous at the house with a tall, red-headed "inmate" named Cecilia Thompson Tunks, 31. Cabbies were valued assets to the skin trade in Key West as they acted as shills for the various brothels when they picked up fares at the railroad terminus and waterfront wharves. For this service they typically received kickbacks of one sort or another.

At any rate, it is lost to history whether it was business, pleasure, or both which motivated Plowman's meetings with the lovely Mrs. Tunks. (Records show she'd married a Navy sailor in October of 1940.)

What is certain is that early in the morning of Feb. 9, 1941 Plowman claimed he got the shock of his life when he went to call on Tunks at her second-floor room at the Reid house. Gliding silently up the rear stairs, Plowman entered the building and knocked at Tunks' door. Receiving no answer, he walked out onto the second-floor verandah and made his way to Tunks' window.

Peering inside, Plowman saw Tunks lying on her bed. He opened the window and climbed down into the room. He quickly realized why Tunks hadn't answered his knock. She lay naked and dead on the bed with a pair of silk panties twisted around her neck with a toothbrush.

Thrown, Plowman slipped out the window and down the stairs. Inexplicably, he walked seven blocks to a downtown bar, and then took a taxi to the police station to report the slaying.

● ● ●

The very next day Justice of the Peace Enrique Esquinaldo called Tunks' death "clearly a murder." Alice Reid and Marvin Griffin were taken into custody as material witnesses along with the bordello's bartender Chester Roberts, as deputies of the Monroe County Sheriff's Office "pushed" their investigation forward, the *Citizen* reported. Despite Plowman's strange actions following his discovery of Tunks' body and the detention of Reid and Griffin, the cab driver remained free, and Esquinaldo claimed to have no suspects in the case.

An inquest begun on Feb. 11, was a "confusing" affair, according to Dorothy Raymer, "with conflicting testimony from nearly all persons involved in any manner."

Chester Roberts told the six-person coroner's jury that he had last seen Tunks in the brothel's lounge around 11:30 p.m. on the night she was killed. One of Tunks' housemates recalled seeing her a little later than that at the bar, stating that all the girls were required to be in the lounge area if they weren't in their rooms dealing with clients.

Photo by roboneal.com

The Howe Street brothel is now a fashionable condo complex.

Auburn Ellis, a steward on a yacht then docked in Key West, admitted that he had gone to Tunks' room with her but had stopped at the bar for a nightcap on his way out.

And Dr. H.C. Galey, who had examined the corpse, informed the jury that Tunks had bruises on her chin and under one eye. How they were caused was a mystery.

Only one person, another of Tunks' housemates, reported any suspicious activity at Alice Reid's that night saying that she had heard what sounded like a heavy person dropping from the low roof outside her window at around 2 a.m.

● ● ●

It was becoming evident that, suspect or no, the case was going to attract a lot of attention from all sorts of law enforcement agencies. It involved sex, violence and the festering issue of the status of the Key West brothels. These establishments were illegal and their presence in the community was an affront to the morals of many people.

Yet others in this Navy-dominated town felt differently.

"When you have a lot of young bucks all together in one small place, whores are a necessity," one indignant Conch told Dorothy

Raymer. "[Without the prostitutes] the sailors will run after our good girls, and women residents won't be safe on our streets."

at tHe tI Me OF tHe cRI Me...

Around 1942, an unknown sailor wrote the following prose titled *Beloved Key West*:

> Key West, oh Key West you moth-eaten town,
> Your unpainted houses should all be torn down.
> Your winters are damp and your summers too hot,
> The air is humid with mildew and rot.
> The land of bad colds, of sore throats and flu.
> Of stiff aching muscles, pneumonia too,
> Your people dull-witted and God, what a bore.
> Your streets are filthy as spring now approaches,
> This materially adds to your crop of cockroaches.
>
> The home of side porches and bumpy thoroughfares,
> With slovenly girls and their awful bland stares.
> You live among roaches and don't mind the rats,
> And all seem to thrive on mosquitoes and gnats.
> You don't speak English, you talk Cubanese,
> Inhaling sewer gas which you think is the breeze.
> You make us pay double for all that you sell,
> But after this war you can go straight to Hell!
> And when you reach Hades and Satan greets you,
> You'll feel right at home, for he's a Key Wester too!
>
> Yes, Key West, oh Key West, it isn't all gravy,
> To be plunked at your feet by Uncle Sam's Navy.
> Have you ever wondered why none of us grieve?
> Why all of us welcome the first chance to leave.
> The worst of it all is you think you are swell,
> You think you are perfect – that gripes like Hell.
> You're rotten, you're dead, and you think you're alive.
> You think you're a place – instead you're a dive.
> You're not worth this paper, you're not worth this ink,
> You can take it from me dear old Key West, YOU STINK!

For now, though, a woman had been strangled to death, and the aftermath wasn't going to be pleasant for the cohorts she left behind.

After three days of questioning by the coroner's jury, Alice Reid, Marvin Griffin and Chester Roberts were all released without being charged.

The authorities were clearly getting nowhere with the Tunks case. The investigation was stalled, with no suspects and no clues.

Back at the Alice Reid house, the proprietor's troubles were just beginning.

On March 4, 1941, the *Citizen* reported that seven women from the brothel, including Reid, had been arrested for vagrancy and were cooling their heels at the Monroe County Jail on Whitehead Street on a $350 bond. They made bail and were once again released pending trial. Life at the house returned to normal - for a while . . .

One week later the house was busted again – this time by the FBI.

In the early morning hours of March 11, at least 10 armed federal agents had stormed the building and rousted Reid, Griffin, Roberts and an unidentified man said to be a Navy sailor. The operation had been conducted under a shroud of secrecy with even local law enforcement officers left out of the loop. It was rumored, the *Citizen* reported, that white slavery charges would soon be filed. Poking around the Howe Street house, a *Citizen* reporter encountered two maids on the property.

"They're all back in jail again," one of them said before being quickly shushed by her co-worker.

• • •

The next day, March 12, it was made official. In addition to the county vagrancy rap, Reid was being charged with violating the federal Mann Act. If convicted she faced five to 10 years in jail. This time bail was set at a daunting $3,000, or over $30,000 in today's dollars.

"Under the elastic terms of the Mann Act, a conviction may be obtained by the federal courts if it is shown that the defendant in any way contributed to the transportation of a woman across the state line for immoral purposes," the *Citizen* explained in its March 12 edition. "Thus, if the women were sent car fare or in any way helped to get into Florida, the act would apply."

By March 14, Marvin Griffin, Roberts, and the unidentified Navy sailor had all been released, uncharged. Authorities seemed to be honing in on Reid, who wasn't having any luck raising her $3,000 bond. She didn't appear to be receiving much help from her husband either. According to the *Citizen*, he had "leased the property to one of the inmates of the house since he was confined in jail."

Yet despite her legal and financial dilemma – or perhaps because of it – she had offered a reward for information leading to Tunks' killer. It was no use. Even with the assistance of the FBI's Washington crime lab, the coroner's jury had by March 25 reported back to Peace Justice Esquinaldo that they hadn't a single clue as to the killer's identity.

"Mrs. Tunks came to her death by strangulation at the hands of a person or persons unknown," was the jury's official verdict. Who had committed the act was anybody's guess.

In mid-April Reid was indicted by a Tampa jury for two violations of the Mann Act, namely transporting prostitutes Margaret Allen and Frances Marchand from Georgia to Key West for immoral purposes. Trial was set to take place in early May at the federal courthouse in Key West.

The Tunks murder, meanwhile, had been taken up by a Monroe County grand jury. During a jury recess on May 6 the *Citizen* reported that a 30-year-old Georgia native named Charles Dewey Faughender had been extradited to Key West from Panama City, Florida, in connection with the Tunks murder. Georgia authorities said that Dewey, who was now being held at the Monroe County Jail, had threatened the life of Tunks before she moved to Key West.

● ● ●

Alice Reid's trial, on May 7, 1941, before Judge John W. Holland, was short and to the point.

According to the *Citizen* report, witnesses testified that "Reid went to a house of prostitution in Atlanta, made arrangements to pay 'Jimmy' Harmon and another man $50 apiece for every woman they procured for the Key West house, and brought [Margaret Allen] here in a car belonging to Catherine Poynter."

In response Reid's lawyers, Bart Riley and Louis Harris, quoted the Bible, Shakespeare, the U.S. Constitution and even Victor Hugo during the stirring defense of their client.

Reid was a "kindhearted woman who had been betrayed by her deeds of kindness just as had Jean Valjean, Hugo's hero in the novel *Les Miserables*," the paper reported Harris as saying.

The defense pointed out that the Mann Act had been intended to keep innocent girls from being sold into slavery, and not to rehabilitate admitted prostitutes. In addition the government's witnesses, including Charles Faughender, Margaret Allen and Jimmy Harmon – who was currently serving time in a Georgia jail – were "thieves from the lowest stratum of society," who were only testifying to have their own sentences reduced.

Mere hours later, the 12 man jury found Reid guilty as charged and Judge Holland sentenced her to three years and four months at a federal prison in West Virginia.

A few days later, after grilling some 35 witnesses the grand jury closed the case on the murder investigation without returning an indictment. They knew Tunks had been murdered but had no idea who might have done it.

● ● ●

With that, the matter was ended. Life returned to normal in Key West – but not to the whorehouses of the Red Light District. Most of the brothels had been forced to shut their doors during the investigation, draining their revenues. Frequent raids from the FBI and now pressure from the city government, which was, in turn, being leaned on by the U.S. Navy, proved to be the coup de grace that closed down many of the cathouses for good.

As the country's participation in World War II approached, Key West-based sailors would no longer be distracted by the established bordellos of Old Town Key West. The venues that survived, such as Mom's Tea Room, were forced to relocate to Stock Island, where they hung on for a decade or so. The days of wide-open prostitution in Key West were over.

● ● ●

Cecelia Tunks never did receive justice.

According to the *Citizen* reporter Raymer, rumors had swirled that the killing had been an "inside job," undertaken by one of the other prostitutes or maybe even Reid herself.

"The motive," Raymer wrote in her *Key West Collection*, "was that Marvin Griffin had been getting overly chummy with Cecelia Tunks . . . there was also a hint that a lesbian element may have been the cause behind the homicide."

The scene of the crime is now a spiffy condo complex called The Galleria, where residents pay big money for their small digs, blissfully unaware of the violent and squalid murder that took place on the very spot they now sit sipping their tropical cocktails.

The mystery of who killed Cecelia Tunks probably never will be solved.

The walls aren't talking, in the bright yellow gingerbread house on Howe Street.

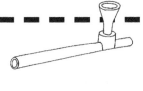

SIDETRACKED BY CRACK

Nearly all the Key West whorehouses, including the Reid/Griffin house were located in Bahama Village, the traditionally black part of town. Recent gentrification and increased tourism has increased property values in the area, but it remains home to some of the cheapest, most squalid housing in town – and the drug trafficking and street prostitution usually found in such areas. A beacon of hope is the Anchors Aweigh Club, located near the corner of Virginia and Whitehead streets. The club offers 12-step recovery programs to those with substance abuse issues.

Courtesy of Monroe County Library
Thomas Overton in court, wearing a stun belt and chains.

MONSTER

A horrific triple murder in Tavernier stunned the community and remained a mystery for years. Finally new technology helped bring the killer to justice . . .

Ask anyone in law enforcement their opinion of DNA testing and the response will probably be immediate and unanimous. It's a godsend. This scientific method, first perfected in the UK in the 1980s, has in the past two decades become an indispensable tool for police and prosecutors worldwide. Its use has helped exonerate hundreds of wrongly convicted criminals in the U.S. alone, but most importantly it's helped seal the case against thousands of other suspects who might otherwise have escaped justice.

This is the story of the first major use of DNA testing in Monroe County – and how it helped solve a dark riddle in the Upper Keys.

● ● ●

Michael James and Susan "Missy" MacIvor were an asset to their tight-knit community. On that all would agree. The young couple moved to exclusive Tavernier Creek in the late 1980s and were well-liked by their friends, neighbors, and co-workers.

Michael was an athletic airplane mechanic who had evidently selected their two-story home for its proximity right next to the Tavaero airstrip, enabling him to fly to work on the mainland almost daily. His wife Susan had graduated from teacher's college at Florida International University early in 1991 and was getting ready to start her first year as a full-fledged teacher at Key Largo School, where she had interned the previous year. Both MacIvors were considered to be no-nonsense type individuals. They ate right, exercised nightly on the landing strip in front of their house, and reveled in the Keys' outdoor lifestyle – often taking to the water in the small pleasure boat they kept docked nearby.

The two were eagerly awaiting the birth of their first child the following month and had last been seen attending a Lamaze childbirth class on Aug. 21.

Given the MacIvors' reputation for uprightness and punctuality, Susan's co-workers became suspicious and concerned when, on the morning of Aug. 22, she failed to show up to meet her new students. Just before noon that day, one of those colleagues went to the MacIvor home and rang the bell.

No answer.

The colleague and a similarly worried neighbor forced their way into the house, where they made a horrifying discovery. The "scantily clad" and motionless body of Michael MacIvor lay bound and gagged on the couple's living room floor. The pair immediately left to call police. A short time later Monroe County Sheriff's deputies arrived at the scene to discover another gruesome find. Susan

MacIvor lay naked, dead, and hogtied with belts, at the foot of the couple's bed.

An autopsy later confirmed that both MacIvors had been strangled and bludgeoned. Michael MacIvor's larynx had been crushed. His wife had been sexually assaulted and semen was discovered on the bed. It appeared that the killer had entered the house through an unlocked sliding door on the second floor and surprised the MacIvors as they lay in bed.

Since the couple's unborn child – already named Kyle Patrick – had been far enough along to be viable, authorities were working the case as a triple homicide, the first such instance ever in Key Largo, according to local LEOs.

The ghoulish killings had shocked the most hardened deputies of the Sheriff's Office. More troubling for them, from an investigative point of view, was the apparent lack of a motive. The cops felt sure, however, that the brutal attack was neither a random murder, nor a botched home invasion.

"The killers probably knew who they were killing," sheriff's spokeswoman Becky Herrin told the *Key West Citizen*. "We don't think this is someone breaking into houses and killing people."

As the investigation ramped up and the parents of the slain family contributed to the growing reward for information in the case, colleagues of the murdered family were left to wonder how such a promising young couple could have met such a tragic, violent end.

"She was one of those gentle people," Susan MacIvor's fellow teacher Karen Dettmann said. "They have that warmth about them, an inner peace . . . the school is devastated."

Aware of just how sickened and outraged by the murders the public was, authorities tried their best to reassure them that they would not rest until the case had been solved.

"We're pulling out all the stops on this one." Monroe County Sheriff's Capt. Joe Leiter told the *Keynoter* newspaper, the day after the killings. "I know how something like this can affect the community."

Yet, it was right about then that the trail grew suddenly cold.

● ● ●

The next five years were difficult ones for the family and friends of the MacIvors. Not only were there no arrests in the case but they were forced to endure speculation within the community that the killings had been the result of a drug deal gone bad, or were somehow Mob-related.

For the first year after the murders, detectives actually worked the case from the narcotics angle, as Michael MacIvor had been in negotiations to purchase a confiscated drug plane from the government of Belize. Investigators even flew to that Central American country to search for clues but came home empty handed. They eventually abandoned their theory and began to focus on Susan MacIvor as the possible intended victim.

"The killer or killers spent more time with Missy than with Mike," Detective Jerry Powell said, in 1992. Profilers agreed the motive could have been sexual. Around this time the crime was reenacted for an episode of the Crime Stoppers TV show with detectives playing the roles of the MacIvors. This move generated a number of leads but nothing that panned out – not immediately anyway.

Notwithstanding the thousands of man hours devoted to solving the murders, the years went by with no major break in the case.

Many observers began to wonder if the killer would ever be caught.

• • •

As the authorities turned over every rock in their frantic search for clues, one man watching from a distance, was sure he knew exactly who had killed the MacIvors and why.

In the spring of 1992 Guy William Green was just another skel serving time for burglary at the Avon Park Correctional Institute in central Florida. Green's burly cellie was another matter. As Green listened to the man discuss his legal dilemma and crime career, Green began to realize that his cellmate was a cold-blooded killer who had yet to be found out.

It was a revelation that would later be revealed at Overton's trial, much to the chagrin of his defense team.

• • •

"We have every reason to believe the killer or killers is still in South Florida," Det. Powell had said in 1992. He was correct. The murderer hadn't gone far.

Among the 30 or so names that surfaced as possible suspects in the wake of the Crime Stoppers reenactment was one Thomas Overton. A 36-year-old career criminal from the south Georgia/ north Florida area, Overton had been in trouble all his life. While a youngster he had been committed to a juvenile mental health center. As a young adult he was kicked out of the Army after two years for stealing a vehicle. Arrested for burglary in the mid-70s Overton managed to escape from a Georgia prison, but by 1980 he was back serving hard time in Pensacola, Florida for armed robbery there. Nine years later, however, his conviction was overturned on appeal and Overton made his way down to the Florida Keys, where he worked as a welder, shoe repairman, diver, and shrimper.

Almost immediately upon his arrival the burly, imposing Overton made an impression on the locals – and it wasn't a good one. He was spotted by police near the scene of a bizarre break-in at a Grassy Key trailer in 1990 but not detained. The target was the home of a 70-year-old woman who returned to find the head of her stuffed parrot twisted off and left on her bed. An accompanying note warned her to get a dog and an alarm and to keep her doors locked.

In January of 1991 Overton took his first collar in the Keys, for driving with a suspended license. Over the next five years, charges of failure to appear, burglary, grand theft, and dealing in stolen property would follow.

At the time of the MacIvor murders the convicted felon – by now working at a gas station the couple patronized – was definitely on the radar of the Upper Keys cops. In the aftermath of the tips generated by the Crime Stoppers segment he became a full-blown suspect. The police even obtained a criminal profile on Overton from the FBI. By the fall of 1996, investigators were itching to bring Overton in for questioning in the MacIvor matter.

Habitual crook that he was, Overton handed the authorities their opportunity on a silver platter. Guessing that their quarry's burglary career was far from over the cops had put Overton under surveillance a year earlier. They also placed a tracking device on his car and convinced a confidential informant to wear a wire while helping Overton work a couple of break-ins.

On the night of Oct. 6, 1996 the moves paid off. Overton, dressed in black and carrying burglary tools and a .45 caliber handgun was busted while trying to steal an antique slot machine from a double-wide trailer in Tavernier.

Courtesy of Monroe County Library

Overton's mug shot.

Following the arrest Special Agent Scott Daniels of the Florida Department of Law Enforcement quizzed the informant for details of the job. What he heard sent a chill up Daniels' spine. Overton, the informant said, had been waiting for the "right weather" to pull off the heist.

"He wanted a downpouring rainstorm," Daniels told the Citizen on Nov. 22, 1996. "He told the informant that in a rainstorm cops don't get out of their cars and it covers up sounds and nobody would do anything."

The heavens had indeed opened and deluged the Upper Keys on that dark night in August 1991 when the MacIvors were slaughtered in their home.

Overton may have been picked up for the relatively minor charge of burglary, but the cops liked the perp for the MacIvor murders and the suspect seemed to sense it.

"Two hours after his arrest he knew he was in bad trouble," Monroe County Sheriff's Det. Sgt. Jerry Powell told the Citizen. "He wanted to deal, so we asked for a blood sample. He said 'No deal, all deals are off.'"

Then Overton literally cut his own throat and transformed the entire case and the future of Monroe County forensics overnight.

• • •

The day after Overton's arrest, police said, Overton deliberately sliced his neck with a razor in the shower of the Plantation Key Jail. The wound from the half-hearted suicide attempt was superficial but the incident sealed Overton's fate. From the towels used to stanch the bleeding the cops had their DNA sample. Overton was moved to the Stock Island Jail where he could be better monitored. The bloody towels were sent to a crime lab for a comparative analysis with the semen left behind on the MacIvors' bed.

The two samples were a perfect match. Following this revelation, investigators got a court order to formally draw an official sample of Overton's blood, just to be on the safe side. The result was the same.

By the third week of November the cops announced that they planned to charge Overton with two counts of first-degree murder, and one count of killing an unborn child due to injuries to its mother. They also suspected him of the murder of 20-year-old Rachelle Surrett, whose battered body was found along Route 905 in 1990. Overton had admitted to investigators that he had a date with the unfortunate woman on the last day she was seen alive but vehemently denied killing her. He also claimed no knowledge of the MacIvor case but given the DNA evidence against him nobody was even listening.

"When he cut his own throat he delivered himself to us," Special Agent Daniels crowed.

Daniels' colleague Det. Sgt. Powell agreed:

"The odds of this [killer] being anyone but Thomas Overton are 1 in 6 billion," he said. "I feel like the fat woman's humming. But she's yet to sing."

● ● ●

A little over two years later, on Jan. 20, 1999, Overton's trial began in the Key West courtroom of County Judge Mark Jones. A jury of four women and eight men, with two alternates, would decide Overton's fate in this landmark trial built partly upon circumstantial – but irrefutable – DNA evidence.

Veteran Assistant State Attorney Jon Ellsworth would prosecute the case. Overton's defense team included public defenders Jason Smith and Manny Garcia. The state, seeking the death penalty, promised to make the proceedings contentious indeed. Towering over his guards, the menacing Overton wore a stun-belt under a thick sweater as color photos of the grisly crime scene were circulated amongst the jury members. Ellsworth took the jury though a chronology of events on the fateful evening, informed them of the DNA evidence against Overton and offered them a glimpse into his backup plan. A former acquaintance of Overton's would relate to the jury details of the case he claimed Overton had revealed to him not long after the murders.

In response, Jason Smith questioned the accuracy of the crime scene investigation.

"This case is based on highly circumstantial evidence," Smith said. "There was no semen on the body, no hair, no blood, no fingerprints, nothing to link Mr. Overton . . . He was an early suspect but when they ran his fingerprints they didn't find anything."

Overton, his lawyers argued, was being framed by the authorities to compensate for their botched investigation.

Several days into the trial the prosecution called a witness whose presence must have made Overton's heart race. It was Guy William Green, the fellow career criminal he'd shared a cell with in Avon Park shortly after the killings.

Green said the accused had described to him a burglary he pulled off in the Florida Keys "at a real exclusive place where the owner parks his plane under his house . . . He said he started fighting with the lady. She jumped on his back and he had to waste her. He called her a fat [expletive,]" Green said.

The defense tried to discredit Green by calling him a jailhouse snitch trying to save his own skin to no avail. It turned out Green hadn't as yet been offered any kind of a deal in exchange for his testimony.

The fat lady was tuning up.

Over the next two days, the prosecution unveiled its DNA evidence, the heart of the case against Overton. It was damning to say the least. After walking the jury though a crash course on the basics of the science Dr. James Pollock Jr., a DNA expert with the Florida Department of Law Enforcement, concluded that "the probability of finding anyone besides Overton with that exact DNA is 1 in 6 billion among Caucasians."

Another star witness, Dr. Robert Bever, was even more certain of Overton's guilt. This lab director and DNA expert for a private company in Virginia used an even more sophisticated testing method to find the odds against Overton to be 4 trillion to 1.

Defense attorney Jason Smith did his best to raise doubts as to the reliability of the state's chain of evidence but again the damage had already been done.

For good measure the prosecution called to the stand yet another cellmate of Overton's, one James Zienteck, an admittedly unsavory character who had been doing time for sexual battery, robbery, grand theft auto, resisting arrest and false imprisonment.

Zienteck swore that, contrary to Guy William Green's testimony, Overton's specific goal on the night of the break-in was to rape "Missy" MacIvor.

The witness claimed that Overton had sneaked into the house and hid in the kitchen as Michael MacIvor, stirring, seemed to sense there was an intruder in his home. Overton swung an iron pipe at the back of MacIvor's head then beat him unconscious with his fists. As the pummeled man began to come to, Overton strangled him to death. When "Missy" MacIvor tried to come to her husband's aid she was beaten, bound, and eventually raped and killed.

As the relatives of the MacIvor family sat stoically in the courtroom, the heavy-set Zienteck, in a quavering voice then revealed information about the final moments of the MacIvor family that left the jury palpably revulsed – and are far too gruesome to be related in this book.

at tHe tI Me OF tHe cRI Me...

The years 1990 and '91 were among the most violent in the history of the Keys. In late September of 1990 Stock Island residents James Alkire and Gregory Gene Cooley were found guilty of savagely murdering two local women and throwing their bodies in the Cow Key Channel. There were both sentenced to life in prison.

The state rested.

On cross-examination, Jason Smith hammered home the point that this particular witness had in fact, received a deal for his testimony. Once again it hardly mattered. Just as it hardly mattered the next day when the defense tried to convince the jury that trace amounts of the spermicide nonoxynol-9 detected in the semen found at the crime scene proved an elaborate frame-up of Overton by the police.

On Feb. 1, 1999 the jury took just two hours to reach its verdict. More than a dozen corrections officers stood guard, grim-faced in the hushed courtroom, as the jury foreman declared that they had found Overton guilty on all counts. Two days later the same jury recommended that Overton be put to death in Florida's electric chair.

On March 18, Judge Jones concurred.

"You have not only forfeited your right to live among us but under the laws of the state of Florida you have forfeited your right to live at all," said Jones addressing Overton and the packed courtroom. "May God have mercy on your soul."

The verdict was immediately sent to the Florida Supreme Court for review as is customary in all capital cases. It would eventually be upheld. In addition to his murder convictions Overton faced numerous other charges relating to his career as a cat burglar. In time he was found guilty of them all. (Florida Keys historian Tom Hambright said the authorities suspect Overton of other crimes, including the shooting a sheriff's deputy in the face, but he has never been formerly charged in the matter.)

By 2012, Overton had exhausted all of his legal appeals and currently sits on death row at the Union Correctional Institute in Raiford, Florida.

He has yet to admit to the killings but thanks to the science of DNA testing there can be little doubt of his culpability.

Convicted murderer Thomas Overton is likely the most vicious, despised criminal in the history of the Florida Keys.

He is, in short, a monster. Soon, he will live on only in nightmares.

May his victims rest in peace.

A DEARTH OF
DEATH SENTENCES

Should Thomas Overton eventually die at the hand of the state, he will become just the fifth or sixth person to be executed for crimes committed in Monroe County since 1830.

An aerial view of Bahama Village today.

BLACKTOWN REBELLION

*The case against accused rapist Sylvanus Johnson
seemed so solid to white Key Westers that a mob
of them decided to forgo a trial and proceeded directly to
the black teen's execution.
Fortunately for community relations here,
cooler heads defused a race riot . . .*

It's been said so often that by now it is beyond cliché. The beautiful Isle of Key West has always had a more tolerant outlook than most similarly-sized towns. It's a perception that's attracted many free-thinking, or liberal-minded folks to the place over the years and become a source of pride for many residents.

Naturally the city hasn't always lived up to these ideals. Early in its history Key West counted amidst its population a number of prominent citizens with what you'd call "mixed feelings" about minorities. (Most of these folks who looked askance at the town's darker-hued citizens were, in fact, small-scale slaveowners who resented the outcome of the Civil War.)

Then there was the case of Manuel "The Islander" Cabeza who was infamously lynched by the local Ku Klux Klan for living with a mulatto woman – and murdering a Klansman – in 1921.

Even so Union troops held the town during the Civil War. Unlike other parts of the Deep South many Key Westers were ambivalent about slavery – and racism in general. Many had moved here from the Bahamas, where slavery had been outlawed for some time.

Nevertheless, black Conchs had to wait until the late 1960s for full desegregation, just like their brethren in the surrounding Southern states.

At any rate, living in a multi-racial port community seems to have more often than not produced civil statesmen from amongst the town's leaders. During the Sylvanus Johnson affair in 1897 every bit of that diplomacy was needed to head off a "race riot" so murderous and ugly that President William McKinley was called upon to intervene.

This chapter recounts how even in an era often considered socially backward from our own, the town's leaders tried to stand up for justice and democracy, though the final verdict was a bitter pill for many in the black community to swallow. Sylvanus Johnson got his trial. But did he get justice? At least one prominent white Key Wester today believes otherwise.

Readers can draw their own conclusions.

● ● ●

The sapodillas were so ripe they were practically dripping from the trees as four young ladies arrived in the wilderness of eastern Key West to pick them. The date was June 24, 1897, and the most pressing issue facing Key Westers that day was likely the hot weather.

This would soon change. By day's end the idyllic snooziness of this post-Civil War tropical paradise would be shattered by a confrontation between the town's blacks and whites. What went wrong?

According to the somewhat inconsistent accounts published at the time, our youthful fruit pickers had been happily gathering up the succulent wild delicacies when they noticed that somebody was throwing rocks at them. They were then taunted by a jeering voice, calling out to them.

Soon after that, they claimed, black teenager Sylvanus Johnson emerged from the dense jungle and attacked them. He first threw himself at Miss Sadie Knowles, who fended him off smartly, scratching his face and smashing his face with her glass water bottle. Next, Johnson went after Mrs. Margaret "Maggie" Atwell, who had come to her friend's aid. While Johnson struggled with Atwell, Knowles claimed, she and the other two women, Miss Emma Ingraham and Mrs. Laura Diaz, quickly made their way to the Atlantic Ocean. Fearful that other men might be hiding in the bushes, the ladies intended to wade down the island to South Beach to get help for their unfortunate friend.

"The negro then turned his attention to Mrs. Atwell," the *Miami Metropolis* reported. "And, after choking her into insensibility succeeded in accomplishing his purpose."

When the three women who had escaped Johnson's clutches reached Key West, an armed posse was formed and the accused rapist was captured somewhere in the area where La Brisa stands today. He was taken before Atwell, who identified him as her assailant.

As word spread through the outraged town Johnson was brought to the county jail in Jackson Square to await his fate. Atwell meanwhile was reported to be ravished to the point of death and as she lay declining a sullen community contemplated the form its required reprisal would take. All over Key West could be heard the sounds of weapons being locked and loaded and as the whiskey passed around voices on both sides of the racial divide grew louder and more insistent.

A respectable white woman was minding her own business, picking fruit, when this nasty brute came along and violated her . . . let's lynch him! That was how many whites felt.

Not without a trial first, came the determined response from the black community leaders.

Predictably a white mob tried to remove Johnson from the jail that night to hang him from a tree, but this attempt was foiled by the jailer Bowers, who refused to disclose to them the combination to the locks. The mob would have to wait until Johnson's arraignment, at 3 p.m. the next day for justice. The blacks would also be watching.

An eerie silence, like the calm before the storm, was reported to hang over the town by stringers sent from newspapers in Tampa and Miami. Simultaneously, over on Eisenhower Avenue a local newspaperman named "Colonel" Chas. D. Pendleton was planning his own, quite explosive appearance at the trial.

The stage was set for a watershed moment in Key West history.

● ● ●

At 3 p.m. the next day Johnson was led into the tense, crowded courtroom of Justice of the Peace J.J. Warren. He was positively identified by several of the sapodilla-gathering women including, once again, Mrs. Maggie Atwell, who claimed that Johnson "threatened to kill her if she resisted" his outrageous intentions. Atwell had apparently recovered sufficiently to take part in the proceedings.

Johnson stood and pleaded not guilty to the crime. He stated that he was out in the woods with four boys, one named Thomas James. He did not remember the names of the other two. James did all the damage, Johnson said, and he had tried to stop him, but being unsuccessful, he ran. "He had never seen James before that day and said that he came from Miami. He had witnesses to offer."

The droning whispers of white anger grew louder and louder until Colonel Pendleton jumped to his feet and hollered "are there enough white men in this room who will help me in lynching this brute?"

All hell broke loose.

With cries of murderous rage in the affirmative the white mob pressed forward cornering Johnson and the closest thing he had to a friend at that moment, Monroe County Sheriff Francis W. Knight, at the front of the courtroom. A similarly incensed black mob took shape on the spot. As pandemonium reigned, Sheriff Knight found himself in the unenviable position of having to physically protect both Johnson from the whites, and a pistol-packing Col. Pendleton, who was now surrounded by a seething mob of Johnson supporters, from the blacks.

As squeamish bystanders fled the courtroom by the dozen, Knight somehow managed to stabilize the situation and Johnson was returned to the jail in one piece, surrounded by a group of armed blacks.

But the black community had been put on notice. Johnson's fellow people of color, who unanimously demanded a proper trial for Johnson, had been forewarned that white enthusiasm for a lynching in this case ran high. If Johnson was going to survive until his trial he would need both help and luck.

* * *

What happened next is somewhat unclear, as the published reports vary, but the gist of it seems to be that on the evening of Johnson's arraignment a posse of blacks broke into the National Guard armory near the jail, and with the weapons they stole, took charge of the perimeter of the lock-up, the armory, and the surrounding streets. They formed themselves into companies for patrol duty and reportedly refused to let white men cross their lines. Mob rule was the order of the day.

Somehow a white man named Willie Gardner, who may have been just passing through the area, was shot in the back and killed leaving his two children orphans. As sporadic shots rang out into the humid night other men, both black and white, fell to the ground wounded. The riot was on. Col. Pendleton, known as a vocal white supremacist both in person and in his newspapers, claimed that his

at tHe tI Me OF tHe cRI Me...

On Feb. 15, 1898, the battleship U.S.S. Maine exploded in Havana Harbor killing nearly 300 sailors. Survivors and the wounded were brought to Key West for treatment and debriefing shortly thereafter. Many of the dead are buried in the Key West City Cemetery.

home had been attacked during the night, but that he had managed to fend the assailants off.

Things were getting serious.

Newspaper reports claimed that entire families were moving to the edge of town to wait out the hostilities. Telegraphs were sent to Florida Governor William Bloxham, who, in turn, informed President McKinley that he feared a full race war in Key West and that he was unconvinced of the ability of local authorities to contain it. The situation necessitated, he said, the use of U.S. Army regulars living in barracks at what is now Fort Zach Taylor, and the U.S. Marines stationed aboard the gunboat Wilmington, anchored in Key West Harbor. The governor had earlier ordered out state militia stationed in the Southernmost City, and had considered sending more from Miami and Tampa. He feared, however, that by the time the soldiers arrived in town the black insurrection might already be in full swing.

Sheriff Knight therefore assembled a posse of about 150 white citizens to help keep the peace and by June 26, with help from the members of the local Company I of the Florida National Guard, the authorities finally succeeded in restoring order in the town.

The race war that President McKinley had taken seriously as a threat had petered out and the U.S. regular troops Gov. Bloxham had requested were never sent.

The Key West race riot had been defused. Now it was time to clean up the legal mess left in its wake.

● ● ●

At least four members of the black mob had been arrested and a reward of $1,000 was being offered for information leading to the prosecution of Willie Gardner's killer.

The arraignment hearing for Sylvanus Johnson, which had been so unceremoniously derailed by Col. Pendleton's courtroom outburst was held a short time later. According to one of the newspapers of the day a "Mrs. Faber" told the court that she, Maggie Atwell and two other women had been gathering "wild flowers" in the woods east of town when Johnson appeared and threw stones at them. He first attacked "Mrs. Faber" before turning his attention to

Atwell, whom he then outraged. What had happened to the "Miss Sadie Knowles" and the others mentioned in the original newspaper reports is a mystery.

Numerous other witnesses for the prosecution followed but the result was a foregone conclusion. Despite Johnson's vigorous denial of the assault on the stand, he was remanded without bail pending the actions of a grand jury.

About a month later the so-called trial of Sylvanus Johnson finally took place. An all-white jury took all of 1 hour and 40 minutes to find him guilty and sentence him to hang. According to author Paul Oritz, writing in his book *Emancipation Betrayed*, Johnson's "court-appointed counsel was not allowed to cross-examine the witnesses. Visibly disgusted with the charade of justice, the condemned man turned to the jury and exclaimed: 'If God was black and came before this jury you would find him guilty. You may hang my black body, but you cannot harm my innocent soul.'"

And hang Johnson did, reportedly singing "Nearer My God To Thee" with his guards as he ascended the scaffold. Johnson maintained his innocence until the very end. The execution was allegedly botched and it took Johnson more than 20 minutes to die of slow strangulation.

Because of this uncivilized legal lynching, and the show trial which preceded it, it's easy to see this as a case where justice was denied.

"The fate of Sylvanus Johnson illustrates the possibilities and limitations of insurgency against lynch law," Oritz writes in *Emancipation Betrayed*. "While armed resistance earned a trial for Johnson, it could not ensure a fair hearing before a jury of his peers."

It's a sad epitaph for a teenager who so clearly understood he was being railroaded.

The casualties were still piling up on both sides however. The family of the murdered Willie Gardner never received proper closure in his case either, according to Monroe County historian Tom Hambright. And the reputation of Col. Pendelton, already suspect in the eyes of the town's moderates, was further sullied. For his part in fanning the flames of hatred, popular Sheriff Frank W. Knight publicly called Pendleton a "drunken egotist getting a little cheap notoriety by a pretense of courage which he did not possess."

Clearly the affair laid bare simmering racial and social tensions in Key West and perhaps also the U.S. in general. President McKinley certainly thought so. Healing the wounds would take time.

As to Ms. Atwell, historian Hambright believes she recovered from the incident and went on to marry and raise a family, though records from the day are sketchy.

He does not believe Sylvanus Johnson was guilty.

"The whole thing is fishy," Hambright said. "This business of the three of them leaving the other one behind with Johnson just doesn't add up to me. Back then, like today, you have boys being boys and girls being girls. When a white woman got caught with a black lover, the lover often became a rapist. I have my doubts about this one . . ."

THE MAYOR WHO CARED:

Larger-than-life fisherman, barman, and all-around character Capt. Tony Tarracino had a well-earned reputation as a man of the people. One day in February of 1990 during his time as mayor of Key West, the controversial shooting of a black man in Bahama Village by white police officers had contributed to racial acrimony in the neighborhood. Tarracino took a long walk around Bahama Village to talk to its residents and assure them the shooting would be

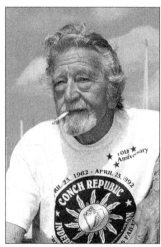

Photo by roboneal.com

properly investigated. The mayor's gambit helped ease tensions in the mostly black area and earned the boozy, skirt-chasing father of 13 respect from all Key Westers. By September the *Citizen* was once again reporting rioting in Bahama Village, due to tensions with police.

Courtesy of Monroe County Library

A Coast Guard reconnaissance boat cautiously approaches the *Seven Seas* on Aug. 8, 1965.

TERRITORIAL PISSINGS

Police agencies sure do enjoy arguments over jurisdiction. Especially when a crime occurs offshore . . .

To fans of TV crime dramas such as Law & Order or CSI, a ubiquitous element of the genre is the territorial pissing match. Just about every episode of top-rated NCIS includes some sort of argument over jurisdiction with local cops, sheriff's deputies, or even other "alphabet soup" federal agencies such as the FBI or CIA. Usually the disputes erupt because each side wants to take charge of the case and/or receive credit for its resolution. Sometimes, though, cases are shifted elsewhere due to the unwanted consumption of precious human and monetary resources that prosecution is likely to consume.

Let's head back to the swinging '60s now for this gory yarn of a murder at sea that ultimately couldn't find a single taker among any of the myriad agencies of the entire, giant squid-like security apparatus of the U.S. of A.

But first, a spoiler alert! For reasons that will later become clear I can't tell you how the story ends . . .

•   •   •

Sunday, Aug. 8, 1965 started off like any other slack day in the Florida Straits for Miami-based Coast Guard patrol plane pilot Lt. Paul Lewis.

As was his routine Lewis and his aircraft set out over the shallow, greenish waters of the Keys searching for any sign of trouble that might necessitate his agency's intervention. An ordinary day on this shift might involve the stranding of a stray lobster boat or a private yacht with a broken mast. For the most part though, surveillance duty in the Straits had settled down into a new kind of normal in the wake of U.S. diplomatic rejection of communist Cuba in 1960. This break with the island's new rulers had provoked a rash of hijackings between the two nations but most of the action was taking place in the friendly skies of American commercial aviation anyway. The maritime-focused Coast Guard plane started out nonetheless.

At about 14:30 hours, Lewis found something to report. A 160-foot cargo vessel was drifting, apparently lifeless, some 36 miles south-southeast of Marathon. The unidentified boat was floating slowly but surely in the direction of the Gulfstream as Lewis made several low passes over this bobbing mystery in the surf.

Seeing no signs of human activity, Lewis radioed his base and soon afterwards the 95-foot Coast Guard cutter *Cape Shoalwater* was dispatched to investigate.

Around 4 p.m. the cutter pulled alongside the freighter, now identified as the Miami-based, Panamanian-registered banana boat *Seven Seas* and blew its whistle.

A short time later, a disheveled man cautiously appeared on deck and yelled out to the Coasties, "The captain has been shot!"

The terrified man then leapt from the bow of the *Seven Seas* to the cutter as a large shark swam along the surface of the water just below him. The haunted-looking sailor was hustled below deck to be interrogated and a heavily armed boarding party clambered aboard the darkened, powerless hulk of the *Seven Seas*. The horror they discovered there belied the vessel's reputation as a "happy" ship, an assertion that was later reported by the press. Three crew members had been shot to death at point-blank range and left to fester in their own pooling blood. In the wheelhouse another large puddle of blood smeared off in the direction of the railing. No other crewmembers, alive or dead, were found.

A full-scale Coast Guard and Navy search of the surrounding area was ordered as the Coasties continued pumping their cryptic castaway for more details. Meanwhile the *Seven Seas* was secured to the stern of the cutter and taken in tow, in rough seas, toward the closest port – Key West.

● ● ●

By early Monday the surviving crewman began to provide details of what had transpired aboard the *Seven Seas*, which had been headed to Tampa from Miami for repairs.

His name was Burywaise Elwin, 17, and in his previous life he had been a farmhand back in his native Honduras.

Elwin told his interrogators of a ship of death; of a murderous rampage by a fellow crewmember which left four of his shipmates dead and two others missing. A 14-foot skiff with two oars that had been fastened to the top deck was also unaccounted for, he said.

The orgy of violence had begun late Saturday evening according to Elwin. He had just finished his noon to 4 p.m. watch and had sat down near the stern of the *Seven Seas* with fellow crewmember Roberto Ramirez, 35, a Cuban national now living in Miami. They spoke of their families and their loneliness at sea.

"He told me about his three daughters in Cuba," Elwin recalled, "and about lobster fishing in Cuba, and how much money he made at it." The subject of Fidel Castro, Cuba's polarizing new communist leader, never came up.

Following the evening meal around 8 p.m., Ramirez joined Captain Rogelio Diaz in the wheelhouse and Elwin retired to the bunk room with some of his shipmates.

A little after 10 p.m. Elwin said he rose from his bunk, unable to sleep due to the intolerable August heat. He decided to try his luck snoozing on deck and made for the portside doorway. Through the gloom Elwin noticed Ramirez enter the sleeping quarters through the starboard door.

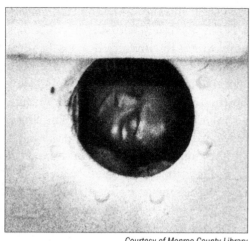
Courtesy of Monroe County Library
A view of one of Ramirez' victims through a porthole.

"He was walking very fast," Elwin said. "He looked right at me but he didn't look mad or anything. I started out the door, and then I heard the first shot. I looked and Roberto had a pistol pointing at the first mate. He had the gun about even with the mate's head and maybe three feet from him. There were two more shots, but I didn't see where he was shooting."

Manic with fear, Elwin scurried up a ladder to the wheelhouse to warn the captain of the carnage taking place belowdecks, but to his dismay the captain himself lay dead in a pool of blood on the upper deck.

Convinced he was next on Ramirez' hit list, Elwin made his way to the bow of the *Seven Seas* and lowered himself into the vessel's chain locker. For the next 19 hours Elwin crouched low in his blisteringly hot and smelly hiding place, praying he wouldn't be discovered and executed by the bloodthirsty Ramirez. At one point Elwin sensed that the ship had changed course and was now headed in the direction of Cuba. Then the engines went dead. Later he heard the sound of the low-flying Coast Guard plane, and eventually the whistle and siren of the *Cape Shoalwater*.

Certain the time had come to make his move, Elwin gingerly crept on deck and called out to the Coasties, who ordered him aboard the cutter for questioning.

A short distance away the *Seven Seas*, rolling gently in the surf, was now a crime scene, stinking of bodies, blood and death. It also bore witness to a mystery. Besides the three slain seamen, Elwin, and Ramirez, three other sailors had been aboard the vessel. The cook, captain and second engineer had all vanished though an explanation had already been provided for the fate of the captain. Elwin told his interrogators he thought the missing cook and second engineer may have tried to escape aboard the ship's skiff.

The gunman Ramirez was also nowhere to be found.

As far as the authorities were concerned, Elwin was the sole survivor of the massacre aboard the *Seven Seas*.

"I'm lucky to be alive," Elwin told the coasties.

No one disagreed.

• • •

at tHe tIme OF tHe cRIme...

In 1963 *Climax* magazine, a racy publication "for men on the go" published a story titled "Orgy at Key West" that had absolutely nothing to do with orgies and everything to do with a touristy, guided bar crawl.

Later that day, the *Cape Shoalwater* neared Key West with its waterlogged charge in tow. In a replay of the 1963 Roger Foster *Dream Girl* case crowds began to gather along Mallory Pier to welcome the blood-stained boat to town. The Coast Guard docks swarmed with dozens of lawmen from various agencies, including the FBI, Customs, US Marshals, and even the Monroe County Sheriff's Office and Key West Police Department. High-ranking brass such as Coast Guard Rear Admiral L.M. Thayer, head of the 7th District, in Miami were also present. The *Seven Seas'* owner Daniel Garcia and some friends and relatives were said to be en route to the Keys to help out with the investigation.

The *Seven Seas* hadn't yet docked but the jockeying for control of the forthcoming investigation was already well underway.

"On the matter of jurisdiction it was brought out that if it is established that a mutiny occurred, it would come under Coast Guard jurisdiction," the *Key West Citizen* reported on Aug. 9. "The FBI would enter the scene, according to information, in the event murder on the high seas occurred aboard a ship owned by an American citizen."

It was also not yet clear to the authorities whether Daniel Garcia held U.S. citizenship, so for the moment the case was one big question mark.

● ● ●

Following the arrival of the vessels at the Coast Guard base Burywaise Elwin led investigators on a morbid tour of the *Seven Seas*, describing, as he went, the events of Saturday night. He first showed the party the wheelhouse where he had discovered Capt. Rogelio Diaz lying dead on the deck and then the trail of blood leading to the railing from which Diaz had been launched down to Davy Jones Locker. A single shoe discovered on the deck was all that remained of the Spanish-born captain.

Elwin then brought the authorities to the steaming compartment, where his three murdered shipmates lay still in their bunks. In their pockets the lawmen discovered a total of $6,000 U.S., adding yet another new wrinkle to the case.

Lastly, Elwin related how he had glanced out at what he surmised to be the lights of Key West before slipping off to hide from Ramirez in the chain locker. It was assumed by the agents that Ramirez then searched the ship for Elwin and that the seaman's quick thinking in finding a safe hiding spot probably saved his life.

Several spent shells, an unfired cartridge from a .38 caliber pistol, as well as a set of oars, and a gassed-up outboard engine for the *Seven Seas'* skiff, were found on deck.

One or more men had definitely set off from the death ship aboard the smaller boat, but whom? The missing cook and second engineer? Or the murderous Ramirez himself? All three?

The Coasties began removing the badly decomposing bodies from the vessel causing one young guardsman to run topside to heave his guts. On land the investigation continued as did the "highly complicated legal matter" of jurisdiction, according to the *Citizen*. For the moment the Coast Guard was running the show at the behest of the government of Panama where the *Seven Seas* was registered. The U.S. Navy, meanwhile, was holding four bodies in its morgue. At the Coast Guard dock officers continued to pump out the more than five feet of seawater that had accumulated in the lower deck of the *Seven Seas*.

"We don't know what we'll find there," said Key West Coast Guard base Commander W.C. Wahl, ominously.

Two questions united the minds of the various assembled lawmen. What had been the motivation for Ramirez' berserker-style attack? And where were the missing sailors and skiff?

Before long, the answers began rolling in, like violent waves against a rocky jetty.

● ● ●

Around 3 a.m. on Tuesday, Aug. 10, the German freighter *Bellavia* was rounding Alligator Reef, about 50 miles north of where the *Seven Seas* had first been spotted, when crewmen heard a cry for help from somewhere out in the dark, humid vastness.

The sailors swung a search beam around the ship and were surprised to discover a skiff manned by a solitary figure rowing in their direction.

Exhausted and dehydrated, Roberto Ramirez was warily hauled

aboard like a tainted tuna and searched. The German crew relieved their unexpected passenger of several knives, a loaded .38 caliber revolver and a baby food jar full of silver-tipped bullets. All that remained of Ramirez' food supply were several soggy pieces of bread. Another day at sea and Ramirez probably would have perished, deepening still further the mystery of what exactly had transpired aboard the *Seven Seas.*

At last the Coasties had their man.

Within two hours, Ramirez was transferred to a Miami-based cutter then on to a Miami Beach immigration processing center. Under the harsh lights of an interrogation room he began to tell his side of the story to a plethora of agents and officers, from every state, county, and federal agency in the book.

● ● ●

Ramirez claimed the whole rampage had been provoked by an argument over the merits of Cuban leader Fidel Castro. Surprisingly perhaps, for a man who described himself as a Cuban exile Ramirez remained a supporter of the bearded revolutionary. (The rest of the crew, save for the politically ambivalent Burywaise Elwin, took the opposing view.)

The ongoing tensions between the homesick Ramirez and the anti-Castro contingent over this issue had come to a head on Saturday night. Unbeknownst to Elwin as he tried to beat the heat in his bunk, Ramirez was up in the wheelhouse arguing about politics with the captain — or so the prisoner now claimed.

As the war of words escalated, Ramirez said that Capt. Diaz threatened to turn him over to Castro-hating Cuban refugee groups in Tampa; he even pulled a knife on Ramirez and ordered him to leave the bridge.

At this point, Ramirez claimed, he pulled out his .38 and shot the captain in a fit of rage. He then killed second engineer Franco Salomon on deck and proceeded to the steaming compartment where he murdered his three other tormentors in cold blood, as they slept. Elwin and the cook, Gerald Davison were spared, Ramirez said, as they had not been involved in the long-running Cuba arguments that had so poisoned the atmosphere aboard. The cook Davison must have then jumped overboard to escape, only to meet his death by drowning in the rough seas. (This part of Ramirez' story seemed to be confirmed when the search of the now-pumped out lower deck of the *Seven Seas* turned up no trace of Davison.) Ramirez then threw Capt. Diaz and second engineer Salomon overboard.

Now at the helm of the *Seven Seas*, Ramirez had steered a course for his homeland, abandoning ship when the vessel appeared to have run out of fuel. As he rowed off in the skiff, only one man remained alive on the *Seven Seas*: Burywaise Elwin.

• • •

As soon as Ramirez finished speaking federal authorities immediately charged him with five counts of murder and one count of piracy. But who exactly was going to prosecute the case? Ramirez was after all a Cuban-born resident alien who had killed people of varied nationalities aboard a Panamanian registered ship that was owned by a Panamaian corporation in turn owned by a Cuban-born American citizen. In addition, the *Seven Seas* had been found drifting in international waters but it was still uncertain whether the killings actually took place in U.S. waters. Plus Ramirez had been in international waters when he was picked off the skiff by the German crew of the *Bellavia*.

What a complicated, messy case!

In fact the file was fast becoming more complicated than a rock musician's love life. As of Wednesday, Aug. 11, the prevailing theory was that since the murders and subsequent piracy took place within sight of Key West the ship was likely in American waters and thus Monroe County prosecutors were entitled to first crack at Ramirez. Given the high-profile and highly politicized nature of this particular litigation however nobody could say for certain what was going to happen.

"It's all up in the air, somewhere over Washington" one federal agent remarked.

How true.

Though the U.S. attorney in Miami was said to be considering a joint prosecution with the Monroe County state attorney the arrangement never materialized. It was rumored that Fidel Castro himself might be heard from, and that the Panamanian government also had indicated interest in prosecuting Ramirez. Ultimately it was the FBI who prepared a warrant charging that Ramirez "feloniously and without authority did take over said vessel and cause said vessel to pursue a course other than directed by its owners, masters and officers, which constitute an offence of piracy, as defined by the law of nations." The warrant also contained the five aforementioned murder charges.

But the grand jury failed to act on the charges and efforts to free Ramirez through a bond or habeas corpus were similarly unsuccessful. Apparently exasperated by the process, the U.S. government dropped its case against Ramirez and in early 1966 extradited him to Panama, a country which had abolished capital punishment upon its independence in 1903.

● ● ●

Given the sensational and incredibly violent nature of the case it's astounding to this writer that the feds would have made any deal that guaranteed that, if convicted, Ramirez wouldn't pay the ultimate price for his heinous crimes. In fact, the U.S. seems to have washed its hands of the Ramirez matter the minute he was carted off to Panama – a situation which bodes ill for those of us curious as to the alleged murderer's ultimate fate. An inquiry made to the State Attorney's Office in Miami yielded nothing but the incredulous statement "that's the weirdest information request I've ever received" from the agency's public information officer. A spokesman for the Panamanian Interior Ministry in Panama was equally unhelpful, diverting my translator Edgardo Alvarado instead to the Panamanian consulate in Miami.

From the staff at the consulate we received tight-lipped advice along the lines of "the only way you're going to find out what happened to this man is to go to Panama and hire a lawyer."

They seemed to know who Roberto Ramirez was or is, Edgardo told me. But they obviously didn't want to divulge what they knew unless ordered to do so by their superiors.

The horrific charges pending against Ramirez makes it tempting to assume that Panamanian authorities sought to put him away for life with no chance of parole.

Truth is often stranger than fiction, though, and in the absence of any real evidence of his trial and conviction – or acquittal – there's just no telling what ultimately became of Ramirez. The American news media stopped reporting on the case following the perp's extradition to Panama. So perhaps Ramirez's family was able to bribe the accused murderer out of a life sentence. Maybe the sailor became a geopolitical bargaining chip in some negotiation with the Ramirez' home country of Cuba. Or it could be that the suspect's messy case ended up tying up the "alphabet soup" law enforcement agencies of that country for so long that Ramirez eventually received a ludicrously light sentence out of lassitude.

Who knows?

I'd sure like to . . .

LAY OF THE LAW

In addition to the Key West Police Department and deputies from the Monroe County Sheriff's Office, Key Westers are also served by the Florida Department of Law Enforcement, the FBI, U.S. and Florida Fish and Wildlife services, the State Troopers, the Department of Homeland Security, the Naval Criminal Investigative Service, and the U.S. Coast Guard. (And those are just the ones we know about!)

Photo by roboneal.com

A dark and stormy night on Washington Street.

A DARK AND STORMY NIGHT

*As wind and rain from Hurricane Ivan lashed the
Florida Keys many residents fled for their lives.
One disturbed young man took leave of his senses . . .*

Aside from a staged hunting "accident," I've always thought that the middle of a hurricane would be the perfect time and place to commit a dastardly crime. Chaos reigns supreme! Police are preoccupied and communications and power are often disrupted; vulnerable people are left to fend for themselves.

The hurricane seasons of 2004 and '05 still rank among the most active in Florida history. In particular, the carnage wrought by Wilma in October of '05 left deep economic and social scars throughout the Keys, many of which have yet to heal.

But a violent incident during fearsome Hurricane Ivan in September of 2004 added a new dimension of terror to cyclone season for storm-weary Key Westers – and changed the lives of a local couple forever.

● ● ●

The howling wind was whipping up whitecaps on the Atlantic and cats and dogs began to whimper and hide as the effects of Category Five Hurricane Ivan began to hit the Keys. It wasn't expected to directly impact Monroe County, but most people weren't taking any chances. Skittish and sensible residents had already evacuated. Only the brave, the foolhardy, and the crazy remained.

The storm had emerged off the coast of Africa in early September and strengthened during its trip across the ocean, becoming a Texas-sized monster and the tenth most intense blow on record by the time it entered the Yucatan Channel. As Ivan's eyewall neared the western tip of Cuba on Sept. 12, that ominous sense of low-pressure dread so keenly felt by animals was beginning to get to some humans as well. Already during the bug-out the Monroe County Sheriff's office had airlifted one Upper Keys stabbing victim to hospital in Miami.

In Key West it truly was "a dark and stormy night" to make purple prose pioneer Baron Lytton proud.

Tim Gallagher, 42, and his wife Lynn Scarpelli, 39, had just finished working a grueling 12-hour shift at the Sands Beach Club, which Gallagher had recently opened with business partner Mark Rossi. As they returned home separately to their Riviera Drive stilt-house, Scarpelli noticed several police cars outside the Bohemia Restaurant in the neighboring Habana Plaza. She paid them no mind, however. Bone-tired, Scarpelli hit the hay, and by 12:45 a.m. was dozing in bed as her husband watched TV in the living room.

Unbeknownst to the couple, the cops had been at Bohemia to check out an incident that would soon affect their lives in a major way.

Courtesy of Monroe County Library

Jan Sykora during his trial.

Earlier that evening Jan Sykora, 28, had been drinking at the bar/restaurant which catered mainly to Eastern European contract laborers such as himself. The undocumented Czech dishwasher had gotten into a fight with another patron and had been kicked out into the stormy night. The police arrived, filled out a perfunctory report, and left.

But Sykora wasn't done yet. He was drunk and angry and returned to Bohemia around 10 p.m. with a tire iron. Sykora swung the tool, and with a sickening thud slammed his earlier adversary in the back of the head. The man's girlfriend tried to intervene but she too was whacked, opening up a cut on her arm. Once again Sykora was booted and the couple was taken to the emergency room. Again the cops came and left.

A short time later as Tim Gallagher sat watching ESPN there was a knock at his front door. The restaurateur opened it but saw only rainy darkness. The puzzled Gallagher walked outside to investigate. That's when the drunken Sykora slipped inside the house. He "grabbed a six-inch filleting knife from a drawer and charged at Gallagher stabbing him five times and puncturing his heart and both lungs," the *Key West Citizen* later reported.

The death struggle lurched its way outside and Scarpelli, hearing the commotion, jumped up to investigate. Seeing her husband's blood in the foyer she ran outside and leapt onto Sykora's back. The assailant wheeled around and turned on Scarpelli, brutally slashing her face numerous times and severing part of her tongue. Somehow Gallagher managed to force Sykora down the stairs, where he stood staring up at the couple.

"He was waiting to see if we were going to die," Scarpelli later told the *Citizen*.

Sykora then removed his pants, cleaned off in the couple's pool and left the property, as Scarpelli called 911. The Key West Police officers dispatched to the scene administered first aid while Gallagher gave them a description of their attacker. A short time later another officer found the bloodied and disorientated Sykora wandering in the street a few blocks from the crime scene, naked from the waist down. Sykora ignored commands to stop and had to be subdued with pepper-spray. Scarpelli identified the madman at the scene and Sykora was hustled off to county jail. The blood-stained filleting knife was also discovered nearby.

Fighting for life, the seriously wounded couple was airlifted to the Ryder Trauma Center in Miami, while the cops set about trying to once again make sense of a crazy, bloody crime spree.

● ● ●

What had possessed Sykora to commit his unspeakable crimes? Investigators searching for a connection between the slasher and his victims kept coming up empty.

Over at The Sands Beach Club, Mark Rossi was also mystified. His friend and business partner Gallagher didn't know Sykora and the latter had never worked at the Sands.

Sykora's former boss at Chili's on North Roosevelt Boulevard was puzzled, calling him one of the "hardest workers" he'd ever employed, a man who always showed up on time and did as he was asked.

It was starting to look like a close friend of the couple was right when she told the *Citizen* that "this was a totally random act of vio-

at tHe tIMe OF tHe cRIMe...

Around 5 a.m. on July 7, 1994 a man snatched a sexy blow-up doll from the Key West Video Store at 528 Duval St. This deluxe model named "Terry" was said to come equipped with a built-in vibrator.

lence that happened to two of the nicest people."

While Scarpelli and Gallagher underwent surgery in Miami, Rossi set about organizing fundraisers for the pair, as well as a blood drive, in view of the amount of plasma they had lost during the brutal ambush.

By Sept. 22 both Gallagher and his wife had recovered enough to leave the hospital and moved into the Fort Lauderdale home of Scarpelli's mother. They were said to be severely traumatized and not ready yet to return to Key West.

• • •

Sykora was already facing charges of attempted murder, armed burglary of an occupied structure, battery of the occupants, and resisting arrest without violence. He was additionally charged with aggravated battery after police located the couple he had attacked with the tire iron at Bohemia. In early October they and another couple from the bar identified Sykora from photos.

Trial was set for March 13, 2006, before Circuit Court Judge Mark Jones. A prison psychologist who examined the defendant said Sykora was depressed, frustrated by his inability to speak English, and stressed out by the hurricane.

Three days before proceedings were to begin the accused surprised everyone – including his own attorney – by conceding his guilt in the case. It was yet another inexplicable act by a strange young man with no apparent rhyme or reason for his actions, but the prosecution was elated nonetheless.

"We are pleased that Sykora chose to plead guilty and avoid a long costly trial and even more trauma for his victims," Chief Assistant State Attorney Catherine Vogel said in a written statement.

On June 10, the convicted slasher sat in court awaiting sentencing. The defense played an hour-long videotape of Sykora's mother pleading for leniency for her son but the moving testimony of Lynn Scarpelli best summed up the feelings in the courtroom.

"I'm afraid to go out at night without my husband. I haven't walked the dogs. I can't taste or feel hot or cold. We have mounting doctor's bills, all because what's his name had a bad day," she said. "Ted Bundy's mother said her son was a good kid . . . a lot of people were stressed about the hurricane, including us, but we didn't go around stabbing people."

Judge Jones sentenced Sykora to three concurrent 50-year stints in prison, stating that aside from murder the crimes in question were the worst he had seen in a quarter-century in the criminal justice system.

The former dishwasher was then led away to begin serving his sentence at the Blackwater Correctional Facility, in the Florida Panhandle.

The town has changed since that dark night in September of '04. The Sands has closed. Gallagher and Scarpelli sold their home and left town. Memories of the incident have slowly faded away.

One fact is certain: The damage Hurricane Ivan left in its wake was unavoidable. The trama caused by Sykora could, and should have been stopped, earlier, on that dark and stormy night.

Photo by roboneal.com

The monument to victims of the Labor Day Hurricane of 1935, in Islamorada.

A MONUMENTAL BLOW

The Labor Day Hurricane of 1935 was the most destructive storm to ever hit the Keys, leaving more than 400 people dead or missing in its wake. Many of these poor souls were World War I vets who had been put to work building the first Overseas Highway. A stylish Art Deco monument to the dead was dedicated on Nov. 14, 1937 at Mile Marker 81.5 of Highway U.S. 1. The bones and ashes of over 300 of the victims are buried in the crypt in front of the monument. Every Labor Day locals gather at the monument to remember the fallen.

A family of herons nesting in the Great White Heron National Wildlife Refuge, on Big Pine Key.

OPEN SEASON

Monroe County Game Warden Guy Bradley went from hunting birds to protecting them with a gun. It pissed a few people off ...

The tiny hamlet of Flamingo bravely faces Florida Bay from its precarious position at the southern tip of Everglades National Park. It's the northernmost outpost of Monroe County and has been an eco-tourism hotspot since the second half of the 20th Century. These days it's little more than a marina and store since its park ranger housing and tourist lodge were destroyed by Hurricane Wilma's floodwaters in 2005.

As the name suggests, it's also a great place for bird-watching.

During the late 1800s and early 1900s however the waters around Flamingo ran red with the blood of birds such as the snowy egret which were hunted for their feathers, used in the making of fashionable ladies' hats.

This plumage was so precious to New York City-based milliners that its weight came to be worth more than gold, leading to indiscriminate hunting throughout South Florida. This brought several bird species to the brink of extinction and conservationists from the recently founded Audubon Society to Tallahassee. Restrictive hunting laws were passed and game wardens were hired.

Among the men who signed on for the unpopular task of policing his neighbors was Guy Bradley.

This is the story of how he came to be America's "first environmental martyr."

● ● ●

Guy Morrell Bradley was born to an educated Chicago family in 1870. The clan moved to Lake Worth, Florida six years later where Guy's father E.R. Bradley worked first as a "barefoot mailman" delivering the post along the beaches from Palm Beach to Miami, and later as the Dade County superintendent of schools.

As an adolescent, Guy Bradley got his first taste of "plume hunting." At the age of 15 he and his older brother participated in a weeks-long Everglades expedition which netted 1,397 individual birds of 36 different species. Guy Bradley had taken to the outdoorsy lifestyle like a wading bird to water.

By 1900 E.R. Bradley had begun working in real estate, and the family moved with him to dinky Flamingo after hearing that hotel and rail bigwig Henry Flagler had decided to run his Overseas Railroad through the area. Flagler later changed his mind and the anticipated land bonanza never materialized but E.R. stayed on anyway as the town's postmaster.

Life at the isolated and mosquito-infested settlement was hard. Many of the pioneers who moved there were loner/misfit-types who eked out a meager existence raising asparagus, eggplant and tomatoes – and by hunting for gator skins and bird plumes. Like frontiersmen everywhere, most had moved to Flamingo to be left alone to live as they saw fit and thus had zero patience for limitations placed on them by "government men." Guy Bradley had grown up hunting and fishing like most of his Flamingo neighbors but his family came from a studious law-and-order background. In time Bradley Jr. began to agree with the consensus growing in the rest of the country that something had to be done to protect wild birds from unscrupulous hunters and hat-makers.

There wasn't much daylight between these two points of view and before long events took place that set the stage for violent confrontations, one of which involved Guy Bradley.

● ● ●

The hunting of wild birds for their plumes for hats had been intensifying since the 1870s and had taken such a heavy toll on the winged wonders that the surviving population had been pushed further and further south, away from major population centers. In Florida, this meant that the largest concentrations of birds, such as the famed Cuthbert Rookery, were located in and around the Everglades, home to all manner of unprincipled poachers.

What's more, this industry which existed to service the fashion scruples of the fair sex, harbored a dirty secret: it was bestial and bloody. Not only were the birds being slaughtered at an unsustainable pace but they were shot or more likely scalped to death during nesting season when their plumes were at their finest and their nestlings at their most vulnerable. This scorched-earth practice led to orphaning of the helpless chicks and was described in 1891 by T. Gilbert Pearson, later president of the National Audubon Society.

"Upon approaching, the screams of young birds reached our ears. The cause of this soon became apparent by the buzzing of

at tHe tI Me OF tHe cRI Me...

On Feb. 5, 1911, Key West Police Officer William Fagan captured a man as he was selling cocaine, the *Key West Citizen* reported.

green flies and the heaps of dead herons festering in the sun, with the back of each bird raw and bleeding. . . . young herons had been left by scores in the nests to perish from exposure and starvation."

By the time of the passage of the 1900 federal Lacey Act, which forbade trade in illegally harvested species such as Florida wading birds, one such hunter was more than ready to hang up his rifle. Guy Bradley.

Guy Morrell Bradley, in the early 1900s.

"I used to hunt plume birds, but since the game laws were passed, I have not killed a plume bird," he told early conservationist William T. Dutcher. "For it is a cruel and hard calling notwithstanding being unlawful. I make this statement upon honor."

By 1901 Dutcher had managed to convince the Florida legislature to pass bird protection laws on the state level but no money was allotted for enforcement. The National Audubon Society decided to pony up the cash to hire four lawmen in South Florida and based on the recommendation of writer and state Audubon Society vice-president Kirk Munroe, Guy Bradley was soon hired on as the official Monroe County game warden. Yet as a former hunter Bradley's enthusiasm for his new gig was tempered somewhat by the knowledge that the new conservation laws were being widely ignored – and that he was about to make a number of well-armed enemies.

"Filled with righteous indignation" and "tough as a red mangrove" Bradley set about his new job with the zeal of the converted. Patrolling a vast area from the 10,000 Islands in the northwest Everglades all the way down the Keys to Key West, Bradley soon became a vilified figure and was occasionally targeted by brigands in the course of his duties. Despite his best efforts to educate area hunters and patrol the areas around the biggest rookeries, the poaching continued, and even increased as the bird populations made a comeback.

It was tough slogging and by July 1903 Bradley moved his family to Key West to get away from the mosquitoes, bad weather - and likely the growing number of death threats directed his way.

The following year a visiting ornithologist Frank M. Chapman made a sadly prescient prediction: "That man Bradley is going to be killed sometime. He has been shot at more than once, and some day they are going to get him."

• • •

On July 9, 1905, Bradley was sitting in his Flamingo home when he heard gunshots coming from the area around the Oyster Keys Rookery in Florida Bay. He jumped in his skiff and set off to investigate. Before long he sighted a vessel belonging to Walter Smith, a known plume hunter and patriarch of a family the Bradleys had known for years. The game warden had arrested Smith's son Tom before, leading the elder Smith to declare "that if Guy Bradley ever attempted to arrest him or any of his family again, he would kill him," according to a tract published by the Audubon House in Key West.

Accounts of what happened next vary, but there's no disputing one fact. Smith shot Bradley, mortally wounding him, before sailing away from the scene of the crime. The slain game warden's body, still in his skiff, was found by his brother Louis, about 10 miles from the rookery. He had bled to death.

A short time later Walter Smith sailed to Key West to turn himself in. He claimed that Bradley had fired at him first with a .32 caliber pistol, and pointed to a slug embedded in the mast of his boat as evidence. Yet Bradley's gun did not appear to have been fired. Also, the dead lawman's family claimed that the bullet that killed Bradley seemed to have entered through his back, supporting their claim that he never would have fired first and had probably been rowing toward Smith's boat with his back to the gunman when the shooting occurred. With no other witnesses to the event, however the authorities felt their case was weak. A jury agreed and the officials declined to prosecute Smith. He was released after spending five months in jail in lieu of $5,000 bond.

The old hunter didn't get off scot-free though. Upon his return to Flamingo he discovered that his house had been burned to the ground, by the brothers of Bradley's widow, some claimed. A short time later he and his family moved away.

"Every movement must have its martyrs and Guy Bradley is the first martyr to the cause of bird protection," said William Dutcher, by then the president of the National Audubon Society. "A home is broken up, children left fatherless, their mother widowed, a faithful and devoted warden cut off in the movement. For what? That a few more plume birds might be secured to adorn heartless women's bonnets! Heretofore, the price has been the life of birds. Now human blood is added."

Upon Bradley's death, no new warden was hired and the carnage soon picked up steam once again. The Audubon Society did buy Bradley's family a spacious house on Carsten's Lane in Key West, where they began a new life together.

In time Bradley's children grew to understand and respect what their father had fought and died for. The "Feather Fight" as it came to be known was finally won by the conservationists with the passage of the Audubon Plumage Bill by New York State in 1910. The act essentially legislated the urban feather markets and plume hat milliners out of existence. Its passage was strongly influenced by the renewal of bird hunting/poaching as well as the outrage which followed the murder of Guy Bradley, his fellow game warden Columbus G. McLeod, three years later, in Charlotte Harbor, Florida, and the killing of Audubon Society employee Pressly Reeves.

Subsequent legislation cemented this political victory. The

open season on Florida's wild birds had finally come to an end.

Guy Bradley was buried in a lonely grave at Cape Sable not far from where his body was discovered. The headstone, which washed away during Hurricane Donna in 1960 read:

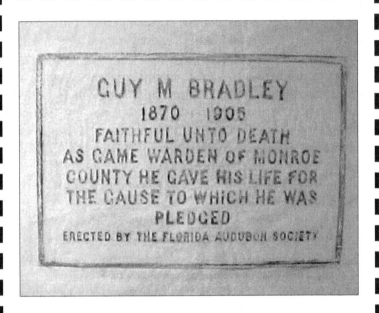

A WATERY GRAVE

Some time after it disappeared, following the 1960 storm, Bradley's gravestone was recovered from Florida Bay and is now on display at the Flamingo Visitor Center. Near the place where Bradley was found dead a plaque was dedicated to his memory and reads "Audubon warden was shot and killed off this shore by outlaw feather hunters, July 8, 1905. His martyrdom created nationwide indignation, strengthened bird protection laws and helped bring Everglades National Park into being."

Courtesy of Monroe County Library

Johnny Ray Holt confers with his lawyers during his trial in 2010.

THROUGH THE CRACKS, DARKLY

The only thing more heartbreaking than a senseless murder is one that should have been prevented. Some say that if the legal system had functioned as it ought to, a patron of Key West might still be alive today . . .

Anyone who knows anything about the law enforcement profession is aware that it's not for the lazy or faint of heart. Rank-and-file cops and their higher-ups in police departments work long hours dealing with seedy and often dangerous offenders. They put their lives on the line to help ordinary citizens on a regular basis.

Even those citizens who diss the authorities will call them when they require assistance. Not all cops are angels, but as a whole they serve a necessary role in society.

As with any profession however, there are incompetents among them who fail in their mission to protect and serve the public. Occasionally these failures are systemic flaws in the legal system itself, leading to catastrophe.

Here's an example of how terribly wrong things can go when the system breaks down.

● ● ●

Rodger Keller was a well-liked, openly gay Key Wester with a talent for gardening and a soft spot for people in need. In fact when the 63-year-old horticulturist moved to the Southernmost City for health reasons in 2001, he brought with him one such needy soul, Donald Hosmer, 55. Hosmer had met Detroit native Keller at the University of Michigan's Matthaei Botanical Garden in Ann Arbor where Keller, a pioneering gay rights activist, had worked for 24 years. When the pair arrived in Key West, Keller rented the man a room at the small house he bought on Fourth Street. The relationship between the two was an uneasy one, though. On Nov. 6, 2005, Keller locked himself in his bedroom and called police claiming that following an afternoon drinking binge, Hosmer had threatened him with an 8-inch knife. The tenant was busted for aggravated assault and taken to jail. Keller initially intended to press charges "because he felt his life was threatened and that Mr. Hosmer would again try to harm him," according to the police report. Before long, however, Keller changed his mind, and Hosmer returned to Ann Arbor alone.

The good-natured gardener remained on the island where he worked part-time at the Monroe Association for ReMARCable Citizens' plant store and also donated his time and considerable knowledge to both the Key West Garden Club and the Key West Orchid Society. He was so well versed on the subject of plants that he was featured in an episode of Home & Garden Television's People, Places and Plants show that airs in occasional rotation to this day.

It didn't take long for Keller to become a highly regarded member of the community. Yet this green thumb maintained his habit of helping people in distress. It would prove to be his undoing.

• • •

On March 23, 2006 Key West police received a phone call placed from a Flagler Avenue restaurant alerting them to a situation at Keller's home. A homeless acquaintance of Keller's named Michael Sox told the cops he had seen Keller pull up in his car and enter his house. Sox then heard a loud "bang" like a gunshot. A short time later Sox saw an unknown man walk out of the home, get into Keller's car and drive off. As the driver stopped at the corner stop sign Sox asked him where Keller was, and was told that the horticulturist was at the "Wildlife Conservatory." The man then drove away leaving Sox to puzzle over what had just happened. Concerned for his friend's safety Sox entered Keller's house through a sliding glass door and discovered what appeared to be blood spattered in front of Keller's closed bedroom door.

Sox immediately went next door and asked construction workers to borrow a cell phone to call police. They declined his request. He then went to another home and asked its occupant – County Judge Mark Jones – for assistance. Again Sox was rebuffed.

Finally Sox was able to get an employee of Lulu's Kiss restaurant to call 911, and the cops were on their way.

Upon arrival police found Keller's body lying in a pool of blood in his bedroom. He had been shot once in the face at close range. It wasn't pretty.

The officers immediately cordoned off the house and set about looking for clues.

The obvious first suspect police considered was Keller's former tenant, Donald Hosmer, but he was almost immediately discount-

at tHe tI Me OF tHe cRI Me...

On July 3, 2006, the *Citizen* reported two separate stabbings in one evening, including one incident said to be motivated by Wicca worship. All parties involved declined to prosecute and no charges were laid.

ed, as he hadn't strayed far from his home base in Michigan. Next, they cleared Michael Sox of suspicion after he passed a lie-detector test.

As the cops worked on alternate theories regarding the killer, locals who knew Keller reflected on the loss of the man they knew as a sweet and giving person, the last type of individual they expected to turn up murdered.

"He was one of the pillars of the Garden Club," the organization's president Rosi Ware told the *Key West Citizen*. "This doesn't happen on this island. This is someone who was well-loved and adored in the horticultural circles."

Another acquaintance, Adrienne O'Brien, who worked with Keller in Ann Arbor, was equally shocked about her friend's death but offered a clue into the reason for his killing: "He had a knack for taking in stray people," she told the *Citizen*.

Before long, the police announced the discovery of their first major clue.

Rodger Keller's green 2001 Honda Civic had been discovered parked on a street about five blocks from Keller's house, and authorities began working it as a secondary crime scene. A police spokeswoman confirmed that the Key West Police Department was investigating multiple suspects and leads.

By March 28 the *Citizen* reported that the prime suspect in the case had been arrested a week earlier in Georgia on an outstanding warrant for a March 17 burglary in Alabama.

His name, Key Westers would soon learn, was Johnny Ray Holt and he had a history with Keller that dated back several years. An arrest warrant for first-degree murder, robbery with a firearm, and burglary of a dwelling – also, while in possession of a firearm - was hastily issued by Key West police so Holt could be transferred back to the island for trial.

Who was this disturbed 24-year-old, and what had driven him to snuff out the life of such a kind and gentle man?

● ● ●

"I love him with all my heart. I was shocked that it could go this far. He had a great personality and everybody, when they first meet

him, loves him to death."
- Jim Holt, adoptive father of Johnny Ray Holt

Johnny Ray Holt was a socially disturbed petty criminal who'd had the police on his back for most of his young life.

He and three siblings were born to a homeless Nashville couple who sometimes fed the family with food scavenged from garbage cans. When Holt was 18-months-old, child welfare authorities put him in a foster home, where he remained until the age of five. At that point both Holt and his older sister were adopted by Jim Holt. Johnny Ray basically learned to speak while trying to talk his way out of juvenile authority trouble.

"He was a smart kid with lots of potential, made good grades, but he had emotional problems from being adopted," Jim Holt told the *Citizen*. "Since he was in foster care at an early age, he didn't have anybody, and he did what he had to do to survive. The first five years are the most important and those things were instilled in him."

Most seriously, Johnny Ray had been sentenced to eight years in prison for the aggravated assault and burglary of a Tennessee co-worker. During that altercation, Johnny Ray broke the man's nose and both eye sockets over a $150 debt.

"He said the guy owed him money and he went to get it," Jim Holt explained.

In 2004 Johnny Ray was released on probation and quickly violated his probation by fleeing the state for Georgia.

From there he moved on to Key West and his first, fateful meeting with Rodger Keller.

• • •

In most places in the U.S., two such disparate souls as Johnny Ray Holt and Rodger Keller would rarely meet, let alone fraternize. But this is Key West, an island of strange bedfellows, both figurative and literal.

According to Jim Holt, his son was working in a bar and sleeping on the beach when he first met "this Mr. Keller, who helps people, homeless people, takes them in; they struck up a relationship."

Before long Johnny Ray had moved into Keller's house. About six months later, on Oct. 24, 2004, Keller told Key West police that the young petty criminal had stolen eight blank checks from him and forged them to the tune of nearly $9,000. An arrest warrant was issued, but by now Johnny Ray had split town.

A short time later the lithe lamster surrendered to the Tennessee arrest warrant for violating his probation, but authorities were apparently unaware of the charges pending against him for check fraud. Johnny Ray was therefore released on probation once again. Even after another arrest in Alabama the young fugitive continued to skate on the check forging charge as he slipped through a crack in the system wide enough to drive a stolen F-150 through.

"Why was he not checked for warrants? There was no Florida warrant for the checks," Jim Holt said. "It never got put into the N.C.I.C. [National Crime Information Center.] If Murfreesboro [Tennessee] did what they needed to do and the [Key West] arrest could have been served, a lot of this could have been avoided."

It was true.

What happened next was that Johnny Ray, by now living in Alabama, borrowed his live-in girlfriend Jennifer Long's car keys and set off, he told her, to "visit a friend." There were other keys on the chain, however, and Johnny Ray soon used one of them to gain entry to Long's parents' house, while there were out of town. There, the troubled young man stole some antique coins, jewelry, two shotguns, a .44 pistol, and the couple's Chevy pickup.

Johnny Ray then drove over 1,000 miles to Key West and, according to police, shot Rodger Keller in the face with the stolen .44. He pilfered Keller's credit card and car, ditching the latter a few blocks from Keller's house. The killer then fled town in the pickup, buying gas with Keller's card and calling phone sex numbers with Keller's cell phone, as he drove north toward the Florida/Georgia line.

Before he left Key West, Johnny Ray had wired Jennifer Long a Western Union money transfer so she could meet him in Georgia, unaware that his girl was by now cooperating with the cops to lure him into a trap. (It seems Long didn't much appreciate Johnny Ray robbing her parents' house with a key she had given him!)

By the end of March, the fugitive was returned to Key West to face multiple felony charges.

● ● ●

An editorial in the April 19 *Citizen* addressed the situation, decrying "the countless ways in which the system failed, most egregiously ... the failure of law enforcement officials in other jurisdictions to hold Johnny Ray in jail on a 2004 warrant from Monroe County."

According to the paper, Holt, while detained by police in Tennessee, flat-out refused to voluntarily return to Florida to answer the check forging charges. However, nobody in Tennessee told Monroe County officials that this violent offender was in custody and would have to be brought back to Key West against his will.

Astonishingly, Johnny Ray had been arrested again, this time for stealing money from his aunt and uncle. He was given a 10 year jail term as a habitual offender. Once again, however, he was allowed out on unsupervised probation.

"In cases like this, it is common to blame 'the system' – but it's worth remembering that the system is made up of people and processes, both of which appear to have failed badly in this case," the *Citizen* opined.

The problem began when a corrections lieutenant from Blount County, Alabama, had erred in telling another county jail to let Holt out, despite the "hold" request that had been issued by Monroe County.

"It was a miscommunication," the officer told the *Citizen*. "I was on my 13th or 14th hour of transporting prisoners."

The paper continued, "It's also worth questioning why the FBI's National Crime Information Center, the database used by law enforcement agencies from different states and agencies to keep track of offenders, is not considered a public record, even though the individual charges logged in there are not allowing public access means there is more opportunity for mistakes and for repeat offenders to slip through the cracks."

● ● ●

In a March 2006 jailhouse interview with a *Citizen* reporter, Johnny Ray admitted robbing Keller but vehemently denied the murder charge.

"I'm not a monster like the media's made me out to be – I didn't kill him" Johnny Ray told the paper.

He claimed that Michael Sox, who also happened to be incarcerated at the Monroe County Jail, (for beating his fiancée with a chair,) was the better suspect. Johnny Ray also conceded that he had been angry with Keller for giving him pills and taking naked photos of him. The cops had indeed found a file in Keller's home marked "Johnny Ray Holt," containing nude photos of his tenant as well as documentation related to the check-forging case.

Initially Johnny Ray had told the cops that he hadn't even traveled to Key West, a lie that was exposed when the evidence of his Western Union transfer surfaced. The police had also discovered Keller's wallet in the back of the stolen pick-up, an incredible coincidence the suspect attributed to a hitchhiker he had picked up.

The suspect's story seemed to be changing almost daily.

● ● ●

Yet the authorities still hadn't finished fumbling the file.

In June of 2007, Johnny Ray Holt filed a federal lawsuit against the Monroe County Sheriff's Office for failing to keep himself and Sox separated inside the jail. The pair had unexpectedly bumped into each other and ended up in a vicious fight the month before, leading to battery charges against Johnny Ray. The action was dismissed in July.

Next, the suspect began a hunger strike to protest his placement in a section of the jail outside of the general population. It was called off after Johnny Ray lost 20 pounds and ended up in the infirmary.

By the time Johnny Ray's trial finally began in September of 2010, the case had already been four years in the making.

The prosecution, seeking life in prison for the accused, began with a recount of the state's considerable evidence.

Defense attorney Jason Smith countered that the shooting had been an accident precipitated by an argument over Johnny Ray's bringing a gun into the Keller home, a violation of the latter's house rules. Smith also tried to blame the victim, suggesting that the friction between Johnny Ray and Keller had also arisen over Keller's "penchant for picking up young, homeless men."

It didn't work.

Two hours after retiring, the jury returned to announce they had found Johnny Ray guilty of the murder. On Sept. 23, 2010, he was sentenced to three consecutive life terms, with no chance of parole, a sentence that was later upheld upon appeal.

Some argued that born loser Johnny Ray Holt never really had a chance at life; others countered that this was no excuse to destroy someone else's.

The system finally did what it was supposed to but not before the needless death of Rodger Keller.

"I don't condone anything he's done and I feel sorry for [Keller's] family," Jim Holt said, "but the foster care system screws up a lot of kids, then the legal system allows it to go on."

It is, authorities say, a systemic problem . . .

GARDEN OF DELIGHTS

The Key West Garden Club and the Orchid Society to which Rodger Keller was so committed meet regularly at the West Martello Tower at White Street and Atlantic Boulevard. This beautiful waterfront attraction was built during the Civil War and contains many species of flowers, plants and insects. The Martello is also a popular place for art exhibits and weddings.

Rodger Keller

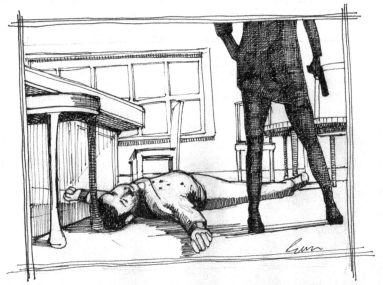

Illustration by Rick Worth

'JUSTIFIABLE HOMICIDE'

Norvella Weaver shot her husband 11 times without batting a green/gray eye, even pausing to reload. The grand jury's verdict? Self-defense!

From 1949 to 1981 Key West writer Dorothy Raymer, mentioned previously in *The House on Howe Street* was a fixture on the newspaper and literary scene. She was a true Key West character with loads of friends in high and low places alike. In the 1930s Raymer had been asked to "withdraw" from Thiel College in Pennsylvania for writing a sociology paper she entitled *Woman Is Not an Incubator*.

Character! She earned her Masters of English Literature from Ohio State University and after a stint at the *Miami News*, made her way down to the Southernmost City in 1949 to work for the *Key West Citizen*.

Raymer retired from full-time journalism in 1977 but quickly accepted an offer from Bill Huckel, publisher of the then-independent *Solares Hill* publication to recollect her Key West memories in a regular column. Several years later Raymer bound these writings into her book *Key West Collection*, which is filled with strange and hilarious accounts from her time as a *Citizen* reporter. Reading Raymer's memoir turned me on to a pair of stories that made such an impression that I decided to research and write about them myself. The two tales are presented back-to-back in this volume as a tribute to Raymer, who died a year after her *Collection* was published.

We begin with this bloody but amusing story about estranged couple Norvella and Tom Weaver.

● ● ●

Around 10:30 p.m. on Aug. 23, 1949 Key West steakhouse owner Tom Weaver waltzed into Weaver's Camp, a Stock Island bar and restaurant owned by his ex-wife Norvella, and sat down in the barroom. This raised eyebrows among the regulars, as it was common knowledge that Norvella had recently sworn out a peace bond against Tom. He wasn't allowed to visit Weaver's Camp under any circumstances.

Before long, Norvella passed by Tom. Words were exchanged and Norvella slipped away to the kitchen. She returned carrying a .32 pistol – and extra ammunition. Wordlessly, she began blazing away at her ex-husband, unloading the gun into him point-blank. As Tom lay on the floor bleeding from six holes in his chest, Norvella calmly reloaded her weapon and proceeded to fire another five shots into her ex, as the bar's many customers looked on dumbfounded.

Her mission accomplished, Norvella calmly sat down in a chair and said "call the sheriff" to nobody in particular.

The law and the ambulance arrived and Tom was taken to hospital where he was pronounced dead. Norvella was taken to the county jail to await a decision by a grand jury as to what charges, if any, would be filed against her.

A *Miami Herald* reporter named David Newton had been tipped off about the shooting and drove to the emergency room in time to view Tom's bloodied body.

"My God! He looks like a sieve," was Newton's reaction.

In the Aug. 24 edition of the *Citizen*, crime reporter Bill Lee stated that Norvella had been "annoyed" by her ex-husband's constant trespassing on her property and had therefore sworn out the peace bond against him. Predictably, the back story was a little more complicated than that.

The very next day, Lee got sauced at Sloppy Joe's, then walked across Greene Street to the *Citizen* to prepare to cover the grand jury hearing into the fate of Norvella Weaver. Unfortunately for the reporter, his long-suffering wife rode up on her bicycle and bashed her husband over the head with her umbrella. With Lee hospitalized it fell to Dorothy Raymer to write the follow-up story, which appeared in the paper the next day.

● ● ●

A carnival-like atmosphere had taken hold at the county courthouse where Justice of the Peace Roy Hamlin had convened the six-man grand jury. Dozens of spectators had jammed both the office where the hearing was taking place and the windows outside.

at tHe tI Me OF tHe cRI Me...

On May 3, 1949, an apprentice seaman named John B. Hollingsworth shot and killed his shipmate Robert Long and pistol whipped another sailor as their vessel sat moored to a pier in the Truman Annex Naval Station. The shooter then hopped off the PC-1263 patrol craft and escaped from the base. He changed into civilian clothes and hired a cab on Duval Street to take him to Boca Chica Naval Air Station. Upon arrival at the gate Hollingsworth threatened the cabbie, Rafael Ferrar with two guns. Alerted cops in the Miami area finally stopped the cab and Hollingsworth was busted. He was flown back to Key West to stand trial.

Raymer took her place outside one of the windows, cringing only slightly as an "enterprising" gawker set up a miniature step ladder beside the window and proceeded to literally breathe down Raymer's neck as the hearing unfolded.

Ice cream and soft drink vendors lined the street in front of the courthouse and made big bucks from the many rubberneckers as the hearing recessed from time to time.

According to Raymer, theories about Norvella's motive were flying fast and furious throughout the crowd.

One man suggested that Norvella was jealous because Tom was such a good cook and that the food at Weaver's Sizzling Steaks was better than hers.

Another maintained that since their divorce Tom kept hassling and threatening Norvella and that as he lay on the barroom floor moaning "help me" she straddled his body and said "now you're really going to get it" before firing five more shots into Tom. One of the bullets reportedly ricocheted and hit a witness in the leg.

Yet another man claimed that the shooting had been sparked by Tom's entering the barroom and depositing 42 nickels into the jukebox that he used to play the song "I Love You So Much It Hurts" over and over and over again.

Many in the crowd seemed to agree that Norvella had purchased her gun on the day of the shooting and spent most of the afternoon target practicing in her backyard. She was teaching herself to shoot "rats" they said.

●　●　●

As the proceedings commenced it was clear there was sympathy for Norvella in the air. Medical Examiner Dr. Herman K. Moore tried vainly to inject a little sanity by testifying that he found no bullets in Tom's corpse because the body had been embalmed before he had been asked to perform the autopsy, but it was no use. The crowd was clearly rooting for Norvella. The room briefly erupted at Moore's revelation before Hamlin's pounding gavel brought the yammering to a halt. Even the judge seemed to have a preconceived opinion on "redheaded" Tom Weaver's temperament.

After the prosecution and defense lawyers had made their pitches, Hamlin asked the six seated "wise men" of the grand jury if they had any questions for either side.

The answer was no, but the jury foreman did ask the judge whether it would be possible to hear Norvella's version of events from the woman herself.

This suggestion raised the ire of prosecutor J. Lancelot Lester who immediately objected on the grounds that the event was only a hearing and not a trial. But Hamlin overruled him. The judge then asked the defendant's lawyers if they had a problem complying with the request.

"My colleague and I would be delighted to have our client testify, if it would clear up circumstances in any way," replied Norvella's Harvard-educated, hot-shot attorney Julius Stone, who in those days was considered the man who had saved Key West from the death grip of the Great Depression.

Judge Hamlin suggested a vote by the jurors to settle the issue, and with that formality out of the way a five minute recess was called to facilitate Norvella's transportation from the jail to the courthouse.

● ● ●

Norvella Weaver, dressed all in black, removed her gaudy rhinestone earrings and took the stand, where she sat twisting a white handkerchief in her hands. The willowy brunette looked older than her 27 years, a condition she claimed in her thick Southern drawl to be the result of Tom forcing her to take "reduction pills."

According to Norvella, her ex-husband was a real creep who had been married several times before he wed Norvella's sister back home in Alabama. After sis died under mysterious circumstances, charmer Tom had latched onto Norvella and eventually made her his wife. Tom then proceeded to beat her, cuss at her, and accuse her of cheating on him at every opportunity. Since their divorce, Norvella said Tom hadn't been supporting their children adequately but had nonetheless threatened to take them away from her out of spite.

At this point Norvella began sobbing.

"My two kids, they come to me and they ask real pitiful-like, 'Mama, how come Daddy don't love you no more?'" Norvella dried her eyes with her hankie as the room buzzed with sympathy. Reporter Raymer noticed one juror wiping his eyes with his tie.

The beginning of the end came, Norvella said, when she finally divorced Tom and not on the terms he had demanded. This infuriated the big bully who began coming around Weaver's Camp regularly, abusing her in front of her customers and telling them terrible things about her. So Norvella had sworn out the peace bond to keep Tom from harassing her. When that didn't work, she returned to the sheriff's office and took out an additional trespassing bond.

Wild with rage, Tom went to the home of one of Norvella's friends and held a gun on her while she phoned his ex-wife. The friend lured Norvella to her home on the pretext of needing a lift from Stock Island to Key West.

When Norvella arrived at the house Tom leaped from the bushes and pulled a gun on her, demanding that she drive him to Weaver's Camp, and also that she drop the bonds taken out against him. They struggled and the gun went off, causing powder burns to Tom's wrist.

Somehow Norvella managed to escape.

The terrified woman immediately went and got a gun permit, the .32, and a box of shells. Only two witnesses of the over 20 that had been present in the bar that night actually showed up, and neither mentioned seeing Norvella shooting at tin cans in her back yard the day of the shooting. Nor did the friend who had been forced to betray Norvella appear to corroborate the defendant's tussle with Tom in her front yard. The jurors were just going to have to take the dewey-eyed defendant's word for it.

Norvella then described their final confrontation.

"When I saw that man come in, I went right to the kitchen where I had hid the gun under a towel. I wrapped it in a fold of my apron, and I went straight back to the bar. Tom went about armed continually, and he was right handy with a gun. I knew he had come out there to kill me that night. When I passed him, he jostled me and said 'This is it!' That's when I shot him."

Prosecutor Lester asked Norvella if Tom actually did have a gun, to which she replied "I don't know. It could have been his elbow, but I wasn't taking any chances. He had a gun that same afternoon, as I done told you. It was either him or me."

Lester shot back with "But why did you reload the gun even after he was already wounded and lying helpless on the floor?"

"Because he wasn't dead yet!" Norvella exclaimed, without missing a beat. "After I shot him for sure I just sat down and said 'call the sheriff.'"

Norvella flashed her compellingly pretty peepers at the jury once more and then sat down next to a perspiring older man – her father.

After about a half-hour of deliberating, the grand jury returned to give its verdict.

With dignified demeanor jury foreman J. Winfield Russell began: "We have duly considered all the facts brought before us. We all agree that this is a case of justifiable homicide, and the shooting was done in self-defense."

The crowd, in and out of the hearing room, exploded with enthusiasm. Norvella sobbed and embraced her father. The pair then went home and presumably celebrated her good fortune over a glass of cheap champagne.

Back at Weaver's Sizzling Steaks, however, the mood was a little more somber. A clueless painter had mistakenly removed "Steaks" from Tom's sign, when his assignment had been asked to remove "Weaver" instead.

According to Raymer's *Key West Collection* "Local wags quipped, 'that's just right! Weaver is sizzling . . . down in hell!'"

As for Weaver's lead attorney, Julius Stone, he had won an unlikely victory over common sense, it would seem. Ironically he figures heavily in the next story we present, titled ● ● ●

PICTURE PURGED

The Monroe County Sheriff's Office retained a photo of Tom Weaver's bullet-ridden body as late as September, 2012, but they refused permission for it to be reprinted in this book. In another loss to history, they also claim that it is likely to be destroyed at some point in the near future.

Courtesy of Monroe County Library
Julius Stone in his office.

...THE MAN WHO SOLD THE WORLD

Julius Stone helped save Key West from the pit of the Great Depression. Then he turned his sights on making money. His business dealings weren't always ethical; they may well have been illegal

K ey West in 1933 was screwed.

The Great Depression had been especially hard on the boom-and-now busted Southernmost City and many voices were now suggesting the unthinkable: that perhaps all involved should accept the inevitable and abandon the town, relocating all the Conchs to the mainland. The situation was so grave that the city fathers handed its sovereignty over to the federal government in exchange for financial aid.

The town was straight-up bankrupt.

Nearly all residents were on relief and many would have starved if not for the abundance of fruit trees and coconut palms on the island, as well as the myriad rainbow-colored fish and plentiful lobster, crab – and conch – to be found in its waters.

Into this morass strode Julius F. Stone, Jr., the Harvard-educated New Deal program administrator. This seeming knight in shining armor had been a paper millionaire before the 1929 stock market crash claimed his fortune, but he had landed safely as a New York State administrator, doing social work under Works Progress Administration chief Harry Hopkins. Following Roosevelt's landmark election Hopkins went to Washington, with Stone in tow. Eleanor Roosevelt had a considerable interest in social welfare and she befriended Stone, recommending him to her husband. Predictably, Stone was parachuted into the driver's seat of Federal Emergency Relief Administration operations for the entire Southeast U.S. and its island territories, including Puerto Rico and the American Virgins.

Through inventive thinking and ruthless, possibly illegal methods, Stone helped Key West turn the corner on the Depression and develop a vibrant tourist industry to bolster the town's feeble economy.

Sadly, this inventive man then turned his sights on development, and became a financier of questionable methods. Eventually it all caught up with him and he left town in a hurry.

Among Stone's many "victims" were Lila Raymer and her daughter, the aforementioned *Key West Citizen* reporter Dorothy Raymer. The younger Raymer wasn't shy about writing about Stone's misdeeds, and dedicated a disdainful chapter of her *Key West Collection* to his exploits. This is fortunate for historians as most of Stone's sketchy maneuverings didn't make the pages of the *Citizen* or other local media. According to Monroe County historian Tom Hambright the marks were too ashamed to admit they had been taken for a ride – or perhaps feared being sued for slander or libel.

● ● ●

Having said all that, it's hard to overstate the debt owed Julius Stone by the city of Key West itself.

The town's very existence hung in the balance in 1934 when Stone made his first visit to the isolated and impoverished island. Like the 12 permanent members of his staff, Stone was aware that the feds were considering throwing in the towel on Key West and evacuating its population entirely. Stone, however, took a liking to the place. In Key West Stone's budding bureaucrat saw its chance to experiment, in a sense, with the idea of completely rebuilding a city – in this case, as a tourist town – from the ground up.

Houses were painted, and sidewalks repaved. Beach cabanas were constructed, and the Navy's sub basin was turned into a marina for visiting yachties. The Key West Aquarium dates from this period as do the few remaining examples of WPA art that can be found around town. Stone even tried to promote the wearing of Bermuda shorts, though this idea fizzled when one irate local showed up to work in his skivvies, stating "if Julius Stone can come to work in his underwear, so can I."

In a more controversial move Stone publicly stated that FERA would prefer that any tourists not willing to spend a full three days in Key West, stay home!

"A shorter trip would be unfair to the visitor and to Key West," said Stone, who was by now being referred to by his admirers as the "Kingfisher," (after the industrious Amos & Andy radio show character,) as well as by his detractors, who referenced the populist U.S.

at tHe tI Me OF tHe cRI Me...

(Keeping in mind that Julius Stone was never actually charged with a crime.)

Hail to the Thief Dept.: During the Democratic primary for state representative, in June 1936, incumbent Bernie C. Papy won reelection after the counting of absentee ballots awarded him an additional 438 votes, and just 16 votes to his challenger, T.S. Caro. The final tally was 1,722 for Papy, and 1,350 for Caro. A Grand Jury was convened but failed to take action on the irregular election results.

Senator Huey "Kingfish" Huey Long, considered a dictatorial dema-
gogue by many in those days.

This brash move could easily have backfired but backed by
prominent Key Westers such as William Freeman and Allen Cleare,
and the directors of the Porter-Allen Insurance Company, Stone's
gambit paid off.

Key West's first tourists began to arrive and the economy began
to recover. By 1935, Stone declared his work in Key West finished. He
left the still-healing town for other government work before retiring completely from public service in 1937. Had the story of Julius
Stone's relationship with Key West ended there, Duval Street would
likely have been renamed in his honor. Instead, Stone returned to
Key West with a newly acquired law degree, also from Harvard, intent on building up his own financial empire. The resulting mess
left many feeling the road to the dump should have been named for
him instead.

● ● ●

Julius Stone's outside-the-box thinking had helped save Key West
and enhanced his reputation. Unfortunately, the methods he used
to accomplish this goal exposed a disturbing authoritarian streak,
one that would later manifest itself in the man's dodgy business
dealings.

In a 1951 interview with the *New Yorker,* Stone admitted that during Key West's makeover he had used federal money to subsidize corporate airline service to the town, and to help get the Casa Marina,
another privately-owned concern back on its profit-pocketing feet.

"With a stroke of the pen I can give it to you – and with the stroke
of a pen, I can take it away," was Stone's Machiavellian signature
saying.

"In following decades," Raymer claimed, "he was to do just
that!"

(Ironically, Raymer's own Masters degree had been signed by
Stone's wealthy father, Julius Sr., who'd been the director of Ohio
State at the time of her graduation.)

● ● ●

The first signs of trouble appeared early on. After being called to the Florida bar Stone went into partnership with fellow attorney W. Curry Harris. Soon, World War II began and Harris joined the service. After the U.S. entered the war, Harris was sent overseas. Upon his return to Key West Harris discovered that his practice no longer existed. It had been consolidated and usurped by "the Kingfisher." Ripping off a returning war vet raised a few eyebrows, but since Harris rebounded and prospered with a new business specializing in deeds and town property, this treachery was forgotten – if not forgiven.

In 1947 Stone and another lawyer, Dine Beakes, tried to develop a neighborhood on a portion of Boca Chica Beach, but the venture failed despite having the backing of Stone's good buddy David Sholtz, governor of Florida. The consortium had gone so far as to tear down the old Boca Chica Bridge before the scheme imploded amidst growing public outrage.

Undaunted, Stone again tried his hand at developing, this time with a neighborhood near Rest Beach. This turned out to be a successful venture, backed by reputable partners.

Stone hadn't turned the corner on Shady Street, though. His office was charging 12 percent interest on loans through a complicated financing mechanism understandable and explainable only by bankers.

In addition to his business conquests, Stone was also making a name for himself as a true legal weasel, with the way he succeeded in securing Norvella Weaver's acquittal at her sensational murder trial being just one example of his courtroom prowess. Stone served as counsel to the Aerovias Q airline operating between Key West and Havana, a grocery store business, a gas company, and more. In the case of the airline he was selling their stock as well – for a hefty commission. In fact, it seemed like charging exorbitant (and sometimes double- and triple-dipped) fees for his investment advice and legal services was becoming his ill-gotten bread and butter.

It was in this capacity, as a facilitator, as it were, of legal transactions, that brought him into business dealings with Dorothy Raymer and her mother, Lila.

In *Key West Collection*, Raymer had this to say about the debacle:

"In 1949 I bought the gift section of Southernmost Flowers and Gifts, then at 616 Duval St. The shop owner was Norval Reed, and Stone was his lawyer as well as becoming mine. Eventually, when Reed left Key West for Miami, he sold the flower shop department to my mother, Lila (Mrs. Earle) Raymer, a widow, and Stone handled that transaction, too! We all paid fat fees for Stone's multifaceted work.

"In 1951, circumstances beyond control (too complicated to go into detail here, including a death in the family and my mother's return to Pennsylvania,) cropped up. At that point, the financial drain for extra help, building repairs, a rebuilt refrigerator for the florist trade, and so on, was too much to sustain without going into debt.

"A new potential client with money to spend wanted to buy the business. Stone put on pressure, and we had to cut our losses and sell at a discount. A banking official informed me later that it was Stone's habit to take advantage of demand notes and to bring about foreclosure on very short notice, not giving a chance for time adjustment."

● ● ●

So it went with Julius Stone.

While administering the estates of dead Key Westers Stone would pile on the fees until, in the words of one victim, the estate "had been administered out of existence." The voracious lawyer always seemed to find a way to keep more than he had earned.

Nowadays this kind of financial chicanery has sadly become the norm, but Stone's antics were taking place amid the backdrop of the healthy, expanding economy of the 1950s. The town's newfound prosperity had been rebuilt from scratch upon the foundations of such New Deal principles as the more egalitarian distribution of wealth, and stricter regulation of financial institutions, to ensure greed never collapsed the system again. Stone's machinations flew in the face of this new conventional wisdom, and a growing number of residents began to resent him for it.

● ● ●

Finally, in August of 1955, Stone's reputation took its first public hit. In his role as counsel to a gas company he had encouraged friends to invest in – again pocketing huge transaction fees – Stone sought an injunction against a rival firm, whom he accused of "tampering with tanks and damaging bottled gas installations." A judge denied Stone's injunction, as well as other claims he had made against the rival gas firm, effectively dealing Stone a full legal defeat.

"The resulting 'scandal' was," according to Raymer, "a discredit to Stone, and more than one person lost invested money."

In another truly shameless move, the social-climbing Stone even began referring to his newly purchased home, next to the Southernmost Point, as the true "Southernmost House in the U.S.A.," even though this caused a schism with his friend and neighbor Hilario Ramos Sr. The latter's palatial lower Duval Street residence had traditionally been considered the true holder of that title. According to Ramos' son Charlie, no survey had even been made to back Stone's claim, and the man himself had admitted that he had designated his house as such, for "commercial enhancement." Ironically, Stone's house already was famous, as the former home of author Thelma Strabel, who wrote *Reap the Wild Wind.* (Today this marquee property is owned by a wealthy member of the Johnson clan, of Johnson & Johnson fame.)

Stone was at the top of the social and economic food chain in Key West, even serving as president of the Key West Art & Historical Society, in 1953-54. Then, over a decade after it began, Stone's empire began to decline.

Much like a traditional Ponzi-type scheme, Stone's secretive business dealings involved acquiring investment money for one thing, then diverting it to another, failing venture. The juggling act was starting to unravel and more people were losing money.

Even Stone's longtime friend and business associate, the respected Judge Aquilino Lopez Jr. severed all ties after learning how distrusted his friend had become by Key Westers.

"My husband was upset and decided that Julius was too much of a dealer," the judge's wife Lilian once said. "He became a judge and was a dedicated man in judiciary matters, while Stone continued to mix law and investment involvements."

More victims piled up.

According to Raymer, other well-known locals who claimed mistreatment by Stone included Frances Edwards, owner of the Banana Tree Grill; Ruth Alfred, who bought the Flame Restaurant and owned a trailer park; Gertrude Ricketts, who operated a private school; and Ethel Decker, a disabled florist Stone bamboozled through property in Mexico; and Dr. Aubrey Hamilton and his wife Belle, who terminated their friendship with Stone after he demanded thousands of dollars from them over the building of a supermarket. The fact that most of these marks were single, vulnerable women, was duly noted by the townsfolk.

At one point, Stone even found some way to milk money from a pair of widows, and this may have been the last straw. By the mid-'50s, federal authorities had opened a file on Stone and were probing his financial operations.

● ● ●

Naturally the ever-inventive Stone had a backup plan prepared. It involved a house in Trinidad, Cuba he and his wife Lee had built in 1955. In 1959, with regulators closing in on him, Stone made it known that he and Lee were moving to Cuba, and they began packing their belongings – and liquidating their assets.

Perhaps Stone had seen the writing on the wall when his colleagues on the board of directors at Florida First National Bank began easing him out of his position in the summer of '59. Meanwhile, Stone continued flying back and forth from Key West to Cuba aboard his private plane, all the while transferring his hard assets to his new safe house. Once that was done, and with Lee safely stashed in Cuba, Stone returned to Key West one more time, to sign over ownership of his "Southernmost House" to a Key West couple. According to Key West lore, Stone may not even have set foot off the plane, preferring to sign over the deed while still on the runway. Other have contradicted this history.

One thing is for sure: this time, in assessing his risks, Stone had completely messed up.

On Jan. 1, 1959, Fidel Castro and his scraggly but determined army of revolutionary "barbudos" had made their triumphant entry into Havana, and this new government had declared its opposition to American economic and political domination of the island. It wasn't a great time to be an American in Cuba, as the Stones began to realize soon after their move there.

Thinking that they might be safer in the capital than in the countryside, the Stones abandoned their Trinidad hideaway, and fled to Havana. There they tried in vain to live with the new reality of communism by opening up an antique store on the famous Prado, but eventually the couple realized there was no future for them in Cuba. They left for Jamaica, never to return. It was there that Lee died in 1963.

For his part, Julius Stone was sighted several times by Key Westers, after departing the rock for good.

Citizen photographer Don Pinder claimed to have had a drink with Stone in a Nassau, Bahamas bar sometime in the early 1960s, and said that Stone told him he was living on an unspecified "out island." He was cagey and didn't sound like he wanted to be found.

Another time, a Key Wester named Ann Carlton ran into Stone in London, England. They got to chatting and Stone told her he had just married Christine Beakes, the widow of his Boca Chica Beach business partner of so many years ago, Dine Beakes. Carlton was delighted, as Christine was an old friend of hers, and she asked for and received the phone number where the newlyweds were staying. The two women caught up over the phone, and the new Mrs. Stone told Carlton they were off to Spain. That was the last Carlton heard of either Stone.

Hilario Ramos told Raymer that Julius and his bride lived on the Spanish mainland for a while, before moving on to the coastal island of Majorca, in the Mediterranean Sea.

From there, the couple moved East.

Julius Stone is rumored to have died of a heart attack in Australia, in 1967. It took the news so long to reach Key West, that the *Citizen* didn't run his obituary until the following year. His only offspring, a daughter named Julia, seems to have fallen off the radar.

Julius Stone led a bittersweet life, and left just such a legacy.

He may not have been the worst thing to hit Key West, but then he wasn't the greatest either . . .

THE ART
OF RECOVERY

During the Great Depression, Julius Stone brought many artists to Key West to help brighten up the town's appearance. Most of the murals and artworks are gone now, but remaining examples can be found in the auditoriums of the now-defunct Glynn R. Archer Elementary School on White Street, and the "Truman School," now the Harvey Government Center, on Truman Avenue. The Key West Art & Historical Society also has several works in its collection, including a painting of Hemingway sitting at the bar at Sloppy Joe's Bar. A similar painting that Sloppy's claims is the original, hangs in the famed watering hole today.

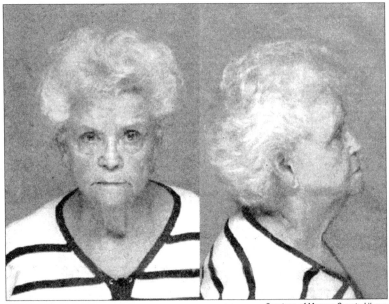

Betty Johnson/Malone/Flynn/Sills/Gentry/Neumar finally faces the music in 2007.

BLACK BETTY

(With apologies to Kurt Vonegut)

Boy, have I got a creepy story for you!

O K, children, all of y'all gather 'round the campfire now, y'hear? I'm gonna tell you the story of ol' Black Betty. She's the one that'll be coming after you later on, if you don't brush your teeth 'fore bed and stuff, see?

So it's like this with ol' Betty.

She was this kinda scary lookin' gal from northern Kentucky way who just couldn't seem to keep a husband. Alive, that is! The craziest thing you've ever seen. Her first man, some fella by the name of Malone, had the good sense to get away from her 'fore anythin' bad happened to him, but then – he kicked the bucket. Then her second Joe, some unlucky sap named Flynn, well then HE went and bought the farm too! Just like that! And this guy was shot to death!

I tells ya, it was a darned good thing for ol' Betty whatsit, Neumar, I think, that nobody was really keepin' an eye on her like they shoulda. Not like they can do with computers and all that nowadays. Because, as the Lord is my witness, what did Betty go and do next? Marry another walking dead man. Can you believe it? A Navy guy in Key West. This one actually shot himself in the chest – twice! With his two stepkids asleep in the next room. Or so the report said. I'll bet you think I'm done now, right? Nope!

Get ready for this: In 1986 or so, Betty's fourth husband was found all shot to death in their living room! Their living room! Sweet Jesus. If I were one of the relatives of one of those poor men, I know I'd a been askin' all KINDS of question, you know? Not sure how she wriggled outta that one!

It's just too bad that one more fella had to have the bad luck to get mixed up with ol' Betty, really. That's this guy Neumar, her FIFTH husband. A sick man. Yup, she buried him too. Well, cremated actually. Without even telling his other family! His own son had to read about his father's passing in the newspapers, same as everybody else!

Anyway, I guess eventually it WAS those computers what done her in in the end. 'Cause after number five died, the cops finally looked up her background and put four and one together to make five, see?! And next thing you know, she's under arrest for hirin' a hit man to kill her FOURTH husband, and they're calling her the Black Widow and all this! They start looking into this Neumar's death a little closer and reopening all them old cases that had been closed or written off as suicides long ago. Her own SON even died of a gunshot wound! Lordy. Some TV crew from the BBC, whatever that is, even made a documentary about Betty. Unbelievable!

Now, I've always been of a mind that one death is one death. But two is a coincidence, three times is a pattern, and four, five times is a Ted Bundy, Jeffrey Dahmer, John Wayne Gacy level serial killer!

Now they had charged her with tryin' to git someone to off her fourth husband, but she died before she went to trial, and before she was charged with killin' them other husbands, but I'll tell you, those kinds of things still leave me wonderin'. . . What are the odds, you know, like they say? And are they even sure that SHE'S dead?

Anyway, let me see if I can remember some of the details about all these poor, dead men . . .

● ● ●

OK, husband number one, Clarence Malone. Now she married him in 1950, right outta high school, but it didn't work out. They were only together about two years 'fore they untied the knot. They went their separate ways, and he married twice more, I think. He gave up the ghost in 1970. Not sure how.

So it goes.

Hubby number two was James Flynn. The cops don't know exactly when they got hitched, but they were only together for three years, 'cause he was shot to death on a pier in New York City in 1955.

It happens sometimes, the cops said. Case closed.

So it goes.

Now number three was an interesting case. This guy, uh . . . Nelos Richard Sills, he enlisted in the Navy when he was 17, in 1948. He was good with his hands, real good, so they made him an aircraft mechanic. He rose up through the ranks to become an Aviation Structural Mechanic, working on these F-4 Phantom jets at the Boca Chica Naval Air Station, in the Lower Keys.

Careful with that marshmallow, child. You're burning it . . .

Anyways, Sills divorced his first wife not long after they got to Key West. By then he already had four kids! You see, Sills drank, and didn't earn a whole lot working for the Navy. His service record had all these letters from creditors trying to collect on cash he owed them. One time, the Navy sent him to the Mediterranean to support his squadron. That, as they say, children, may have been the straw that broke the back of his first marriage.

So one day, Sills meets this Betty Flynn lady, a divorcee and widow working at Martin's Hair Salon on North Roosevelt Boulevard, and who's got these two kids of her own. They hit it off, and next thing you know, he's married her and moved into a trailer on Big Coppitt Key with Betty, her daughter Peggy, and her son Gary.

Courtesy of Monroe County Library

Betty, center, with daughter Petty, right, and son Gary, in 1967.

By now, things were looking up for Sills. I guess his life with Betty in the trailer was stable and he was looking forward to receiving a Navy pension and rejoining the civilian workforce, where they paid way better than the Navy back then.

At the same time though, Sills was still drinking, and he had gained a lot of weight, probably from all the stress from his divorce, and worrying about money all the time.

So, Sills asked the Navy for permission to transfer to the Fleet Reserve, basically a way for him to retire before his enlistment was up. They said no. I guess they needed him, what with Vietnam starting to heat up. Vietnam. You know, I never did understand that one. Huh. Vietnam . . .

Anyways, I guess we'll never know what the conversations were like in that trailer up on Big Coppitt, but I'll betcha they was gettin' louder and alouder.

One night, April 18, 1967, I remember the date, 'cause I was living in the Keys in those days, Peggy Flynn woke up to this huge, loud argument between her stepdad, and her mom, Betty. They had been out drinking and were carrying on like two dogs in a sack, with their bedroom door closed.

Suddenly, Peggy heard this loud BANG! Or maybe two, she couldn't remember, and she ran into the bedroom, to see her step-dad, all bloodied up, lying on the bed. They rushed him to the hospital, but he died on the way.

So it goes.

Ol' Betty, she told the cops that Sills had shot himself with a .22 pistol. The bullet had pierced his heart, and sliced his liver. He must have been a heckuva shot! Either that, or there was more than one bullet, which wouldn't have looked good for Betty. Still, the very next day, the Sheriff's Office ruled the death a suicide, and Black Betty became a widow for the second time.

Less than a week later, Betty had Sills buried in an unmarked grave at a cemetery in Ocala, even though the Navy would have paid for a headstone.

Then she went and collected Sills' death benefits from the Navy disbursement office. One cool cucumber, our Betty. Didn't miss a beat.

In fact, the very next year she went and jumped the broom again! This time, the vic . . . er, the husband, was this guy Thomas Harold Gentry, who actually preferred to be called by his middle name. Now, they stayed together a long time. I guess it seemed like he could be her soul mate. Why, he was even there to console her when her son Gary blew his own head off with a shotgun. She must have been devastated. 'Course, then she turned around and collected $10,000 from her son's life insurance policy, so I guess there was some kind of a silver lining. Betty even told the cops her son wasn't married, but he was . . . married with three kids!

So it goes.

Anyways, one day in 1986, Betty came home to find her husband

at tHe tI Me OF tHe cRI Me...

On Jan. 2, 1986 the *Citizen* reported that the Coast Guard had intercepted three vessels carrying more than 16 tons of marijuana between them. Some 17 smugglers were arrested in the non-related trafficking operations.

Harold Gentry shot up like Swiss cheese at their place in Norwood, North Carolina. Fortunately for Betty, this Gentry had a $20,000 life insurance policy, with her as the beneficiary, that musta helped take the sting out of his untimely death. That kind of cash could have lasted her for years!

So it goes.

This time, however, there was a new wrinkle for the four-time widow: Gentry's brother Al had grown a little wary of Ol' Betty, and he urged the cops to take a closer look at the case. Eventually this came back to haunt her.

In the meantime, though, Betty didn't look back. In 1991, she married her final husband, John Neumar, and settled into a life of domestic bliss with her one-and-only.

That was a joke, kids, a JOKE. Get it? Domestic bliss? Black Betty? See how that works?

Actually, this Neumar fellow managed to survive living with Betty for 26 years, not quite a record, but respectable all the same. Still, even he wasn't immune to the curse. When he died in 2007 the cause of death was said to be sepsis, ischemic bowel, and ileus – symptoms, I'm told, that could have been from arsenic poisoning.

So it goes.

In fact, Neumar's son John Jr. was immediately suspicious of Betty. He told the cops that he found out about his father's death by reading his obituary in the newspaper. He called Betty and was told she had cremated him, even though Neumar had already bought a burial plot!

Well, this was the beginning of the end for Betty's run of bad luck with men. Neumar's ashes were seized and tested for arsenic poison, but none was found. Nonetheless, Ol' Betty was busted in 2007, on suspicion of arranging her fourth husband's murder. Someone had tipped off the cops that she had been casting about for a hit man, and Betty, by now a grandmother, was finally under investigation. In May of 2008, she was shipped off to North Carolina to face three charges of trying to pay a neighbor, and also a retired cop, to kill Harold Gentry for the insurance money. The deaths of the other husbands were now being reinvestigated, excluding Clarence Malone, her first, but including that of Richard Sills, whose family found out about Betty's arrest, from some reporter who had gotten wind of the story. Sure enough, the press started calling Betty the Black Widow, and they made that documentary film I was telling y'all about. The producers even got an interview with Betty, the only one she ever gave.

In the summer of 2008 Sills' son Michael reached out to the Monroe County Sheriff's Office, as well as the Naval Criminal Investigative Service, which began trying to figure out whether or not his dad's death really was a suicide. Michael Sills also struck up a long-distance friendship with Al Gentry, who was also awaiting a resolution to the case of his late brother Harold.

Unfortunately Richard Sills' autopsy report had gone missing, and the statute of limitations on second- and third-degree murder had already expired. The authorities wanted to dig up his body, but that effort went nowhere. The State Attorney dropped the matter, so the Sills case is still considered a suicide.

In fact, aside from the murder-for-hire charges involving Harold Gentry, none of the other investigations were really producing results, beyond plenty of sensational newspaper and television coverage of the case. Betty was out of jail on a $300,000 bond when SHE finally met up with the Grim Reaper in a Louisiana hospital on June 13, 2011.

So it goes!

Betty may have taken some terrible secrets to the grave, but I guess now we'll never know. It looks that way, anyways. Still, after her passing, the cops said they'd be looking into Betty's death certificate . . . just to be on the safe side.

I mean, they SAY she's dead, but you never know . . . some people can be slippery as eels. Betty might just have been one of them! She was only 79. Still had plenty of time left to find true love . . .

OK kids, the fire is out. It's past your bedtimes, and the story is over. Y'all be good and go to sleep now, or Black Betty's gonna come back and get ya!

So it will go.

IN THE NAVY

Key West may have lost most of its Naval presence over the years, but on the bright side, life is easier for servicemen and women than in Richard Sills' time. Today pay and benefits are often higher than in equivalent positions on the private sector. Additionally, many Navy families living on base enjoy homes on the water, with docks and boats to take advantage of the fabulous Florida Keys outdoor lifestyle.

Illustration by Rick Worth

TWO WOMEN FIGHTING
OVER A VIBRATOR
ON FRANCES STREET

When I first moved to Key West in 1995 the following story had been recently reported in the *Key West Citizen* and was making the rounds at all the bars and cocktail parties. Two years on, when I became the paper's crime reporter, people would mention it to me whenever I introduced myself as an employee of the "Mullet Wrapper." And some time later when I decided to write a book about true crime here I was besieged by this question wherever I went: "Does it have the one about the two lesbians fighting over the dildo?" The very idea of the story crystallized, for me and many others, the frivolous, flamboyant side of Key West we moved here to enjoy, so I really wanted to include it in *Vol.1*. The problem was, I'd never actually read it, and due to issues with the *Citizen*'s (ahem) archiving system, wasn't able to track the story down. Reluctantly, I let it go and moved on.

Two crime books later, however, public enthusiasm for this little nugget hadn't waned, so I vowed to finally unearth it and include it in this edition. With the help of an acquaintance who had held on to a copy of the original story, I'm now finally able to do just that.

It's a little light on details, as *Citizen* Crime Reports from the early 1990s rarely included dates, times, or names of minor offenders. I've also had to rewrite it, for copyright reasons but here, for the first time in paperback, is the story about "the two lesbians fighting over the dildo."

- T.S.

● ● ●

Something was in the air – or drinking water – that evening, as Key West Police officers John Elmore and John Beuth responded to reports of a domestic dispute at the Brass Key Guest House on Frances Street.

at tHe tI Me OF tHe cRI Me...

Early in the morning of Sept. 29, 1994, two tourists discovered the bloody, beaten body of Blue Lagoon Motel night auditor Wilbur R. Patterson. Four suspects were ultimately charged in connection with his slaying. Arturi Verra, who struck the blow that killed Patterson, was convicted of first-degree murder, and sentenced to life in prison. He too, was murdered, in prison, three years later. Bradford Downey, a juvenile at the time of the murder, went inside the hotel with Verra. He pleaded out to second-degree murder, and was sentenced to 17.35 years in prison, as well as probation afterwards.

Downey's girlfriend, Amy Tuite, acted as a lookout. She agreed to testify against the others, and was sentenced to 51 months in prison, for robbery.

And Jeff Arnold, Jr., who also acted as a lookout, also agreed to testify. He was sentenced to 60 months in prison for robbery. He is currently back in jail on unrelated charges.

Upon their arrival, the two cops physically separated two Fort Lauderdale women who were arguing loudly with each other. The reason for the tourists' disagreement soon became clear. The younger of the two, a 20-year-old, was angry that her older partner, 28, had stolen her $90 vibrator and was running off with another woman.

"The stamp-on deluxe model was purchased by me at Trader Tom's in Fort L. from Kevin," the young woman wrote in her report to police. "Kevin can describe the model and the fact that I purchased it for me." She also claimed to have a receipt for the sex device in her truck, but never actually went to retrieve it.

For her part, the older woman claimed her partner had given her the vibrator as a gift. She said the two of them had been staying at the guest house, but her vibrant younger friend had become enraged when she brought another woman back to the room. The older woman was ready to leave, with her bags packed when the bemused cops arrived on the scene.

The younger woman, who was clearly the more agitated of the two, also accused her former friend of trying to steal her credit card, but a search of the older woman's bags failed to turn up that bit of plastic.

As the questioning continued, the younger woman became so vexed that she kicked a can of soda out of the older woman's hand.

The police, who obviously missed the training class on dildo disputes, concluded that the argument was a "civil" matter, and allowed the older woman to leave with her new girlfriend – as well as her older, plastic friend.

• • •

As an addendum to this story, the years following this incident have seen so many sex toy-related crimes and incidents that it has become near-impossible to keep track of them all. For instance, In March 2011, a Marathon man was arrested for burglary after his ex-girlfriend handed over to the police a box of sex toys her ex had stolen from a nearby trailer. She claimed that he had brought them home to her in January saying he had stolen them nearby as a "souvenir" for her. The sex toys were indentified by the rightful owner, and the suspect was charged with criminal mischief, burglary and theft.

Only in the Keys!

"DILDO ISLAND"

Dildo Key is a small, uninhabited island in Florida Bay named after the Dildo Cactus (Acanthocereus Tetragonus,) a native species.

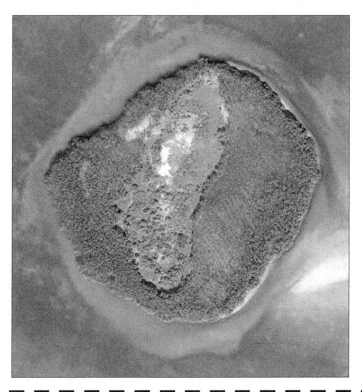

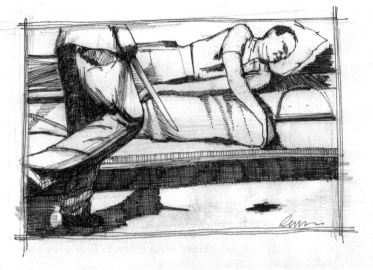

Illustration by Rick Worth

VIOLENT PARTNER

Astute Midwestern businessman Duane Rath
was known for his innovative corporate governance,
philanthropy and modest demeanor. His "other half,"
Frederick Hurdman, could be hell . . .

In a quiet, peaceful garden next to the Key West Library on Fleming Street sits a silent testament to the generous spirit of a man Key Westers barely got a chance to know.

V. Duane Rath was a highly successful Midwestern manufacturer of stainless steel tubing products who, from the time he was a teenager, helped his parents build a near-bankrupt company into a thriving national concern. In the early '90s though, Rath had sold the Janesville, Wisconsin-based company in order to focus more intently on his greatest passion in life, helping people.

With his life partner Frederick "Ted" Hurdman in tow, Rath traveled the country spreading his wealth liberally among those he considered neediest – always insisting on downplaying the role he personally played in such generosity.

Rath also always believed that charity began at home, with worthy people and projects in Janesville.

Attracted by the weather and lifestyle of Key West, Rath and Hurdman, a strapping former Green Beret, found their way down to what was then a gay mecca. They set about enjoying their vacation home here while Rath, true to form, looked for opportunities to contribute to the community.

The local library was at that time searching for funds to refurbish a decrepit piece of property on its grounds and so presented one such opportunity to the industrialist. Rath's behest to the Friends of the Key West Library was gratefully accepted and put to good use.

Yet, whatever pleasure this good deed may have brought Rath he wasn't able to enjoy it for long. You see, the multi-millionaire carried with him a terrible, nagging, secret: His relationship with Hurdman was a stormy one, with flashes of rage, and occasional physical violence – and it was escalating.

Rath never lived to see the full fruition of his gift to the library. The details of his demise are grisly, and though his death did not take place in the Southernmost City, its reverberations were felt all over the country; it's still a Key West tale.

This is the sad story of how the Key West Library – and thus the town itself – lost a friend.

● ● ●

The problem was always the same.

Whenever the Rath Manufacturing company went to purchase the stainless steel tubing they required to manufacture farm machinery at its Janesville plant, it was hard to come by and subsequently more expensive than it should have been.

"When the market was in very short supply," Duane Rath later recalled in an interview with *Forbes Magazine*, "we would call certain vendors for estimates and they would literally laugh at us."

It was the mid-1970s and the family-owned corporation Rath presided over was about to undergo an industrial revolution of its own.

The firm had begun under a different name with the purchase of a bankrupt farm equipment manufacturer in 1952, and had seen more than its share of ups and downs over the years.

Rath family patriarch and business brain, Virgil Rath, sold milking machinery and had one day bought out a supplier, hoping to achieve through hard work and innovation the success that had eluded the original owner. Unfortunately for Rath, the business turned out to be more competitive than he had originally anticipated, and a year after the acquisition, the company was barely in the black. By the next year, with a mere $600 in the corporate kitty, the senior Rath very nearly threw in the towel.

Then something amazing happened.

In 1954, Virgil's 16-year-old son V. Duane Rath, still in high school, took over as sales manager and began an aggressive push to make the business a success. Like a scene from the 1995 road buddy flick "Tommy Boy," Duane Rath began traveling far and wide in a Plymouth convertible, tirelessly peddling the company's wares. A born salesman, Rath continued his sales pitches, even as he completed an English lit degree at the University of Wisconsin.

For his graduation present, Virgil Rath promoted his son to the post of president. The enterprise, now known as Rath Manufacturing, began to grow. At one point in the early '70s, progress was delayed when the Rath plant burned to the ground, but through perseverance and diligence the resilient Rath family managed to pick up the pieces and start over.

By the time Duane Rath bought out his parents interest in the company for $112,000, in 1975, Rath Manufacturing was well on its way to becoming a regional economic titan. Realizing that the chronic shortage of steel tubing presented a huge opportunity, the Raths had revolutionized the process of producing it, and shrewdly made it the focus of their production. Business was on an upswing.

It didn't hurt that the Raths had wisely bought labor peace with their employees through a management plan that left them non-unionized but working largely unsupervised, with flexible hours and a generous bonus scheme. Everybody in town wanted to work there.

By the late '70s, with manufacturing in decline across North America, Rath Manufacturing was bucking the trend, building a new state-of-the-art plant in anticipation of better times ahead. This optimism was not misplaced. Sales surged from $6 million in 1984 to nearly $45 million, five years later. Rath Manufacturing had arrived.

● ● ●

Obviously, Duane Rath was an unusual boss.

Not only did he treat his employees as equal partners in running his company but he made himself available to them, always willing to lend a hand with whatever personal problems they might be having.

"My philosophy is one of shared stewardship," Rath told the *Milwaukee Sentinel.* "I don't believe I own things."

At Rath Manufacturing's 1989 Christmas party, Duane dressed up as Santa Claus and announced that he had decided to personally pay for five-year college educations – including room and board – for the children of all 125 of his employees. It wasn't just the punchbowl talking. The Rath president soon established the Rath Foundation, charged with overseeing the scholarship program, so that it was sure to outlive Rath's association with the company should he sell it – or die.

Countless other charities and non-profits had already benefited from Rath's largess: AIDS organizations and hospitals across the country; the Washington Holocaust memorial. One time he quietly paid for a heart and lung transplant for a 15-year-old Janesville boy whose devoted but low-income family learned their mysterious benefactor's identity only upon his death.

Over the years, all this giving led Rath to cross paths with A-list celebrities such as Elizabeth Taylor, with whom he opened an AIDS clinic in Washington D.C. Having made it in the business world, Rath was now a successful philanthropist.

In 1991, at the age of 50, Rath sold his company, intending to spend the rest of his days with his partner Fred Hurdman, giving away the fabulous fortune he had worked so hard to earn.

There was just one problem. According to friends, Rath and Hurdman had been having major relationship difficulties.

"They weren't good together," one woman told the *Janesville Gazette*. "Ted had a very violent temper, because I know how he was with me."

Outwardly, at least, the ruggedly handsome Rath was all smiles. In the background however, lurked Hurdman, a man with a hair-trigger timbre, who had been trained by the U.S. Army to kill people in a silent, almost casual fashion.

• • •

Exactly when or where Duane Rath first met Ted Hurdman is unclear, but it appears they became an item shortly after the latter moved to the Janesville area, around 1980, to work for Parker Pen. A graduate of Southern Illinois University, Hurdman had served in the U.S. special forces in Panama, doing God-knows-what. After leaving the military, Hurdman had traveled extensively through South America, eventually sailing by himself to Hawaii. By the time he ended up in Janesville, he had tired of living in crowded places and was seeking a quiet place to raise and show horses, his great love in life.

In Duane Rath, Hurdman had hit the jackpot. Together the couple lived a life that the *Advocate* magazine described as "their own gay version of 'Lifestyles of the Rich and Famous.'"

In addition to Rath's 13-acre estate in Janesville, complete with horse stables, the couple bounced around from properties in Mineral Point, Wisconsin., Telluride, Colorado and, of course, Key West.

• • •

at tHe tI Me OF tHe cRI Me...

On Nov. 8, 1994, the *Citizen* reported that a local angler had hooked 20 kilos of cocaine while fishing a half-mile off Islamorada, Oceanside. The packages were turned over to the Sheriff's Office for analysis and destruction.

Rath had spent his formative years in stifling, socially conservative Janesville, so relished the openness and laissez faire attitude of Key West. Hurdman would probably rather be riding his horses somewhere on the mainland but the couple began spending more and more time in the Southernmost City regardless.

For a time, they lived in a condo in the tony William Fleming House complex, before purchasing a million dollar mansion at 51 Front St., in the city's gated Truman Annex community.

Soon Rath was cutting checks again, this time for the purchase of a dialysis machine for an area hospital - and to help build the Palm Garden at the Key West Library.

For the latter endeavor Rath donated a cool quarter-million bucks.

A photo of the grand opening of the new garden which ran Feb. 15, 1994, in the *Key West Citizen*, shows a smiling Rath blending neatly into the crowd. As usual, the philanthropist hadn't wanted any public recognition for his deed.

In fact, few people in Key West had any idea who Duane Rath was until Oct. 6, 1994. That morning a groundskeeper discovered the blood-soaked body of the affable millionaire in the bedroom of his Janesville mansion. He had been brutally stabbed a dozen times with large kitchen knives. In the garage the employee found the body of Fred Hurdman, who had apparently taken his own life by breathing in carbon monoxide.

An apparent suicide note, the contents of which the cops refused to divulge, had been left nearby.

● ● ●

The murder of Duane Rath, who had done so much for so many, provoked a national outpouring of grief from those whom he had helped most. Jim Graham, executive director of the D.C.-based Whitman Walker Clinic spoke for many when he told the *Advocate* "It is a loss to our movement of profound proportions. The gay and lesbian community has no one with the capability, the willingness, and the enthusiasm that Duane shared with gay and lesbian causes. There are a lot of people with that kind of money, but I don't know of anyone else with his kind of commitment."

While news of the murder-suicide may have come as a shock to the outside world, those in the couple's inner circle, accustomed to the lovers' many quarrels, were half-expecting it.

"This does not surprise me at all," said one woman who had worked as a horse-groomer at the Janesville estate. "I can remember [Ted] running at me across the pasture, just screaming and swearing. He scared me to death. I could not wait to get away from him. I left because of Ted," she added.

Exactly what had triggered the final confrontation between the two men remains unclear. Unnamed sources told the *Janesville Gazette* that Rath had recently taken a new lover and may have been planning to cut Hurdman loose from his $20,000 per month allowance and other perks. Rath had even considered hiring a bodyguard to protect him from his own lover, in the event that Hurdman took the news of his rejection poorly.

Authorities also hinted that the note found at the crime scene contained a reference to a horse farm Hurdman had wanted to buy near Tampa. Rath, friends said, had refused to pay for it. Ironically Hurdman was listed in Rath's will, and would have received a "major portion of Rath's estate," including the Truman Annex house, had he himself not been dead - and responsible for his lover's death, the *Key West Citizen* reported.

Whatever the reason for the tragic turn of events, the bottom line is that a good man was killed, and nothing can bring him back.

Yet Rath's one-time gift to the city of Key West remains a considerable legacy.

The Palm Garden, which Rath's donation did so much to bring about, is today more than just a quiet place to read, or meditate under shady trees. It is a venue for the Friends of the Library's monthly book sales and other fundraising events, which bring in considerable revenue for this important local institution. In these cash-strapped times, such revenue has helped make it possible for the library to operate without reducing services or hours of operation.

So, from those of us who rely on the library for our livelihoods, enjoyment, and education, and perhaps for the generations yet to come, thank you Duane Rath.

The world needs more people like you.

YOU'VE GOT TO HAVE FRIENDS

The Friends of the Key West Library was formed in 1972 with a mission to "support, improve and promote the Key West Library through fundraising, volunteering and raising public interest in the library and its services. For more information about this dedicated group visit http://friendsofthekeywestlibrary.org/

Above, the library's Palm Garden, to which Rath contributed $250,000. Below, the plaque noting Rath's contribution to the site dedicated June 4, 1994.

Photos by roboneal.com

CORRECTIONS/CLARIFICATIONS

This book is a work of non-fiction and every care has been taken in the research process to reflect accurate accounts of these historical events. Should you have compelling evidence to suggest that factual errors have been made in the telling of these stories, your input would be welcomed, and used in the editing of future editions of this book.

GUILTY PARTIES . . .

If writing this book was a true crime I'd have lots of accomplices. (Far too many to prosecute, I reckon!) Medellin Cartel overlords would be Mom and Dad. Thanks, guys for encouragement, financing, and editing help, as well as for your love and "protection."

My consigliere is, sans doubt, Tom Hambright. The man cherishes history and sharing it with the rest of us. Bless you, my friend!

Underbosses include Rob O'Neal, Wesley Sizemore, Rick Worth and Stephanie Hellstrom. Lieutenant Club donors number Tom Corcoran, Michael Haskins, Craven Morehead, Danette Baso Silvers, Edgardo Alvarado and Jane Marter. Other syndicate members include Becky Herrin (ssssh!), Gregg McGrady, and in Wisconsin, the staff of the *Janesville Gazette*, and the Janesville Public Library. Canadian affiliates include true crime guru Max Haines, and fellow book lover Amy Cormier.

Cheers to David Sloan for help with the early development of this series and a shout out to Tricia for music, friendship, and "Slaughterhouse Five." Meow to Fergles, who watched while I wrote. Danke! to Achim, for technical, and moral support.

Special recognition goes to crime reporters Frank Jacobson, Wendy Tucker, Marc Caputo, Adam Linhardt, Traci Rork, Kip Blevin, Richard Hatch, Chris Tittel, Jim Tucci, and all the other names behind the anonymous bylines, for laying the groundwork for many of these stories.

There's a little of all of you in this book . . . Thanks!

Terry Schmida

The author gratefully acknowledges the financial support of the Anne McKee Artist Foundation.

ABOUT THE AUTHOR

Photo by Peter Arnow

Terry Schmida moved to Key West from Canada in the summer of 1995, with dreams of becoming a newspaper reporter. Since then, he has worked at the *Key West Citizen* as a writer, editor, ad-maker, and columnist. *True Crime Vol. 3* is his third book.

GET VOLUMES 1 AND 2

Don't miss the other two titles in the *True Crime* series! Both are available at bookstores, online at www.amazon.com or directly from the author by emailing keysscribe@aol.com.

THEY'RE ARRESTING!

Photo by roboneal.com

"This is the end," sez Bigfoot.

Made in the USA
Las Vegas, NV
30 April 2021